Rafa

in

Rhyme

Juliette Westbrook-Finch

Since my last book was published I've donated some money to 'The Rafael Nadal Foundation' because if I hadn't been so inspired by Rafa's attitude on and off the court, this book (and my previous two) would not exist!

Watching Rafa on TV, I became an admirer of him as a player and a person which led me to look him up on the internet and find his website. I put some of my poems about him on the forum to share with other fans who enjoyed reading them: their encouragement as well as following Rafa's example to never give up is what led me to get my work published.

I believe that the chain of events that led me from watching my hero on TV to being a published author is no coincidence: it was part of my life purpose; my soul's plan, and my spirit guides were working behind the scenes giving me a nudge, making me feel drawn to Rafa, knowing he'd inspire me and lead me in the right direction!

I think it's interesting and amazing that a hero can inspire you to make your dreams come true even if his/her dream isn't the same as yours; if it wasn't for Rafa I would have just carried on writing for my own amusement but instead I have surprised myself and done something that I never thought I could!

First published in the United kingdom in 2016
By Emocionado Publishing.

ISBN 978-0-9565266-3-2

Contents

Acknowledgements

Thanks to Rafael Nadal for inspiring me to write 3 books and for touching so many people's lives in a positive way, for inspiring me to never give up and make my dream a reality like he has.

Thanks to Jess and Carol for all their help in making this book a reality and helping me to accomplish my dream.

Thanks to my friend Trisha for coining the phrase 'Rafaland' when she sent me a postcard from Mallorca, I've used that in the descriptive poem on the back cover.

Thanks to my lovely parents for their love and support and for giving me these creative genes, I love you mum and dad, and my husband Martin for putting up with my love for Rafa!

Introduction

This collection of poems was written from approximately 2006 onwards and are a poetic history of some of Rafa's most memorable matches as well as a poetic tribute to his life on and off the court.

This book contains the Rafa chapter from my 2 previous books, 'The Poetry of Passion (for People with a Pulse)' and 'The Poetry of Passion Part Two (for People like You)', as well as many new poems that are exclusive to this book.

Since watching Rafa lose to Federer in the 2006 Wimbledon final I started to look him up on the internet on a regular basis, and I joined the forum on his website: the more I found out about him, the more I admired him. He inspires me and has helped me get through some tough times.

A hero brings out many feelings in their fans: love and admiration, feeling protective and sticking up for their hero and comradery with other fans; a hero really enriches your life, they can bring like-minded people together and inspire people to follow their dreams.

If my hero is your hero, you'll identify with my poems. I hope you enjoy them......

Chapter One – Magnifico Matches

This chapter is a poetic history of some of Rafa's memorable matches and there are also some poems about his matches in general.

It also includes a poem for each round when he won The French Open and Wimbledon in 2010. These wins hold very special memories for Rafa fans due to the fact that in 2009 he lost the French Open in the 4th round to Soderling (after winning it for 4 consecutive years from 2005-2008) and had to pull out of Wimbledon, so was unable to defend his title (which he won for the 1st time in 2008) for the same reason – due to injured knees; he was also coping with the breakup of his parents' marriage at that time so 2009 was a very difficult year for Rafa.

Rafa fans are very protective of their hero as he is such a nice person so the fact that he lost to Soderling made it all the more terrible because he had previously tried to humiliate Rafa on court at Wimbledon (because he was losing and was obviously trying to put Rafa off) by ridiculing him and his mannerisms. Rafa kept his concentration and won the match; when asked about Soderling's actions afterwards he said, "It's not nice, in the end we will see what's happening in the end of the life, no."

Magnifico Matches

This chapter's called 'Magnifico Matches'
and we've seen more than a few of those:
every match that Rafa plays,
his determination and willpower grows.

His body language stays eager and positive,
his concentration stays focused on the job;
the artillery of shots he can choose from,
range from dropshots to volleys to lobs.

He's amazing from the baseline
when he hits one down the line,
and gentle volleys up at the net,
well, his 'hands' are just sublime.

He's a genius with a racket,
I'll never tire of watching him play;
his shot making and topspin speed
will take him all the way!

Animal Passion from Magical Mr. Nadal

He had the sexy saunter of a confident assassin,
and as he ran around the court
he hit each shot with passion;
hungry like the wolf
and eager like a beaver,
it's all coming together
like he's just switched on a lever;
fast and ferocious, confident and calm;
and don't ya just love it when he flexes his arm!

Look at his face: he's so in the zone,
it won't be long before his rival's sent home;
he bounces around effortlessly:
as agile and strong as he could be;
aggressive attacking, circular motion:
topspin forehand like a magic potion;
intelligent serving with calm focus,
a recipe that needs no hocus pocus;
his game is magic, just as it is:
this man really is the biz!

A Man with a Mission

Animated expressions,
confident impressions,
body language determined,
fast as a whirlwind;
a man with a mission,
for the trophy he's wishing.

Beautiful movements,
still making improvements,
smarter and sharper,
accurate and faster;
more talent than the rest,
for sure he's the best!

Good Luck to Our King of Clay (2008)

Three French Opens in a row,
you're better than Federer and he knows:
the only reason he's still Number One
is results he got before you'd begun;
and as for Novak, you've tamed him too,
you're so in control, there's naught he can do.

So tomorrow on court when you face Fed again,
you'll break him down and continue your reign:
your talent and strength will have him floored –
but I wish you luck with each net cord!

(I knew you'd win, you are the best,
you're definitely a cut above the rest!)

Class on Grass (2008)

After winning the French
you came straight to the Artois,
you've proved yourself on clay,
now you've done it on grass;
tough opponents,
you've faced them all:
and one by one
you've made them fall;
you're the hurdle
they can't overcome,
you've proved you're the best
with this winning run.

Ready for Wimbledon (2008)

Last year at Wimbledon you came so close,
but this year you can make the most
of the fact that you've got them all psyched out:
they know you're the best, of that there's no doubt.

You stopped Roger's run at Hamburg in May,
you beat Novak on grass as well as clay:
you showed them at Queens just how good you are,
you're on a roll – you're the best by far!

You'll win Wimbledon with class and style
and show the world, you're the best by a mile.
(and he did)

The Greatest Final Ever (Wimbledon 2008)

The last 2 years Federer beat you in the final,
each time I shed a tear;
but now you've just won Queens on grass:
I think this will be your year!

The match was just amazing;
the greatest of all time,
it spanned 7 hours and 5 sets with 2 rain delays;
the tennis was sublime.

You won sets 1 and 2,
I was so thrilled and excited for you:
I felt sure you'd win it in 3;
but against Federer, that wasn't to be.

Federer took set 3 on a tiebreak,
I wasn't too worried just then;
but when he took set 4, my heart it sunk,
'Rafa don't let him beat you again!'

The rain and the loss of set 4 didn't dampen your spirits;
you still told Toni you were gonna win it:
you were so much calmer than him,
and determined to get that win.

It got darker in the final set:
how they saw the ball was a mystery,
but Rafa pulled off an amazing win
in the greatest game in History!

This year was 3rd time lucky for you

after being runner up the last 2 years;
6-4, 6-4, 6-7, 6-7, 9-7
is the score that gave us happy tears!

Vintage Nadal

Vintage Nadal in 2008,
you'll go down in history as one of the greats,
you've got all the players so psyched out:
they know you're the best, of that there's no doubt.

In Monte Carlo and Barcelona you continued your run,
four in a row twice, a job well done;
you stopped Roger's run at Hamburg in May,
four French Opens, you're the 'King of Clay.'

At Queens in June, you beat Novak on grass,
then you won Wimbledon with style and class:
after forcing your rivals into submission
you deserved time out for rest and fishing!

Next in Toronto you set your sights
on winning again and you reached great heights:
to be Number One, the chance you grabbed it,
beating Federer's becoming a habit!
Olympic Gold, you won that too,
no one deserves it more than you.

A strong macho warrior who's gentle and kind,
a more beautiful person you'll never find;
a stylish leader, the one who sets trends,
you're grounded and loyal to all your old friends.

Your kindness and consideration
created 'The Rafael Nadal Foundation,'
you make the world a better place,
as a tennis player and a man you are just Ace!

I'm wishing you luck for 2009,
with talent like yours, I know that you'll shine;
I admire your devotion to keep on improving,
you deserve the success that devotion will bring.

Your tennis is exciting and full of action,
no one else gets a hotter reaction:
when you walk on the court
your charisma shines through,
so many people feel drawn to you.

A Spanish accent and a smile so sweet,
no wonder ladies fall at your feet!
You're a modest Hero who's humble and shy –
you really are a special guy!

Amazing Aussie Semi (2009)

I want you to win
as much as you do,
I'm emotionally drained
but I'm glad you pulled through.

A roller coaster ride
is where we have been,
a tiring match
but a win you did glean.

Now take some time
to rest on your bed,
so you're fresh as a fish
when you take on Fed!

Aussie Champ 2009

Rafa, your wish
and ours came true,
when you won in Australia:
we're so happy for you.

The wish that you made
on the dandelion seed,
really helped
you to succeed!

You're a true champion
on and off the court:
the kindness you showed Federer
can't be bought.

A deserving winner
with compassion that's true:
you're the best role model,
that's why we love you.

Rafa's the Ferrari

If Raonic tries to psych you out,
ignore his blarney,
your body's fine tuned
like a sexy Ferrari!

As you put your foot down,
you're in complete control,
speeding along to reach your goal.

You got the moves, you got the speed,
that opponent of yours better take heed;
try as he might, he'll run and dash –
but playing you, his game's a car crash!

Davis Cup Victory (2009) Vamos Spain!

Rafa, I'm so happy to see the bull is back,
playing like a genius,
you're so on the right track:
psyched up with tennis flowing,
confidence is growing,
momentums started flowing,
now you'll keep on going –
like a runaway train,
you're unstoppable again!

I'm sure it will continue,
there's so much fight that's in you;
you'll carry it through to 2010
and win the Australian Open again!
Keep on vamosing –
it's you that we love watching!

Can I just say
that you looked beautiful today:
poetry in motion, full of devotion,
skillful and artistic, amazingly quick;
the 400th win of your career,
another winning run is starting here!

Indian Wells (March 2010)

Your 3rd round match was a joy to see:
close to perfection, I think you'll agree;
in the driving seat, that's where you were,
some miraculous shots, I was watching occur;
you're great to watch when you're playing like that,
if you don't win, I'll eat my hat!

That's what I thought and I was right,
you gave us a lesson in tennis tonight:
complete control, strength and power,
any short balls, you devour.

You played each point with mucho gusto,
your game's working right and you go with the flow,
it looked so natural and right for you,
that's what I feel, did you feel it too?

Then you were interviewed on Sky TV,
you made me laugh, you're so funny;
those shorts won't be around next week:
it sounds like they'll be up the creek!
(on a slow boat to China maybe?!)
You said you liked them on paper
with their check design,
but not in the 'real;'
you won't wear them next time!

Rafa on the Red Stuff

Now the clay season is starting,
your CV you'll be enhancing,
adding titles left, right and centre –
no one could have a better mentor:
to follow in your footsteps,
many dream of;
you're the one we admire and love;
so good luck Rafa, although you won't need it,
you're talent alone will make you a hit,
but I'll send you good luck anyway
and hope it helps you when you play.

Rafa on the red stuff,
the fans can't get enough,
the other players, he's surpassed,
his matches are over oh so fast:
his record on clay is the best you'll get –
and he's not even finished adding titles yet!

Winner Monte Carlo (April 2010)

Those who said you're finished must eat their words,
doubters and critics are a load of nerds!
Your true fans always knew you'd do it:
no one can stop you when you're fit.

Rafa on clay, strawberries and cream:
some things go together like a dream;
automatic, systematic;
for his opponents it's problematic!
Dynamic, dynamite:
that's why the trophy, he will bite:
and all his fans will be high as a kite!

You let your tennis do the talking,
now it's the others that are walking
off the court, as they have lost,
now you've shown them you're the boss!

I knew the trophy he'd be biting,
our 'King of Clay' just keeps on fighting;
now he's won Monte Carlo 6 consecutive years –
he's breaking records and going up the gears!

Ready to Peak (Barcelona)

Congrats Rafa, you're in the final again,
'Vamos' tomorrow, I hope the outcome's the same

as it was last week when you won in Monte Carlo,
you'll win Barcelona if you go with the flow;

you're gaining momentum, getting ready to peak,
at just the right time, at the end of the week;

the trophy's polished and waiting for you
to take a bite like you always do!

Super Semi in Rome (May 2010)

Full of zest to complete your quest;
Gulbis gave you a difficult test:
(it nearly gave me a cardiac arrest!)
but you came through with flying colours,
you're much stronger than the others:
strength of body and strength of mind,
a more determined opponent they'll never find:
no matter how good they are, beating you's unrealistic,
they've only gotta check the statistics!

If you were nervous it didn't show:
you still looked strong and ready to go;
when things didn't go your way
you never got down,
you stayed calm and strong
and your tennis was sound:
you hit amazing shots with talent and ease,
you bring your opponents to their metaphorical knees.

Your fans are excited and very delighted,
you're back to your best and your passion's ignited –
mine is too, I want you to win with a passion:
my feelings are strong; they cannot be rationed.

You run round the court speedily dashing,
all your outfits start a brand new fashion;
there's so much your fans want to emulate,
our 'King of Clay,' you're just *so* great.

Style and talent, positive attitude,
these are qualities that you exude;

that's why I want to be like you,
you inspire me so much
with all that you do.

You never give up, you keep on working
towards your goals, never shirking:
you do all you can to follow your dreams;
to be a success; as so much it means.

Setbacks made you stronger,
you kept on trying:
now the rewards are coming,
you're back and you're flying;
your rivals know it too;
they've seen your rise,
you've stopped all talk of your demise:
they know you're the best
when you're fit and on clay,
that's why our King's reached the final today.

Psyched, Sexy & Skilled (Madrid 13/5/2010)

You look so sexy when you're all psyched up,
Isner's window of opportunity was soon slammed shut:
running cross court or down the line,
skill and accuracy every time;
when you talk to yourself with enthusiastic gusto,
you look so hot the ladies feel such lusto!

In Masters titles you've tied with Agassi;
but that's not where you'll leave it be,
you'll surpass that record with the skill you've got,
your body's not the *only* thing that's hot;
your tennis is too, it's really on fire,
you'll be climbing the rankings, higher and higher.

You're the one we love to see,
when you win, we're in ecstasy!
LOL, but Rafa it's true,
we've all fallen in love with you!

The Best Man Won (Madrid Semi 15/5/10)

In the 1st set you just couldn't get it together,
losing serve 3 times didn't help your endeavor,
but you broke his too, so only lost it 4-6,
by the 2nd set your game was solid as a brick!
(which is just as solid as a rock!)

You saved break points and held your serve,
you broke his too and held your nerve;
you took the 2nd set by 6 games to 2,
the final set beckoned, you knew what to do.

You were on the board 1st
with a good service game,
then you broke Almagro's –
you got him tamed;
it started off as a difficult match,
but you turned it around
and brought your game up to scratch:
cool and calm, patient and poised,
to grab your chances when they arise:
you took the last set 6 games to 2,
the best man won –
Rafa that's you!

Mallorcan Matador Wins Madrid (May 2010)

Spectacular hitting, speed and control,
Federer couldn't stop you reaching your goal:

intelligent tactics, played with calm;
I was 'Vamosing' and flexing my arm:

watching the best, you play with finesse;
your tennis did the talking, into history you're walking:

the first man to win 3 masters on clay,
you've sent your rivals a message today:

woe betide them, if they meet you at the French,
you're thirsty for success,
and that thirst you will quench;

so today in Madrid, it's a job well done,
you've made history – you're on a winning run!

Primeval Instinct

Heightened senses,
eyes of a hawk;
very close call:
challenge or walk?
Primeval instinct,
move in for the kill;
hunt your prey:
hit winners at will.
Crucial point,
honed and ready;
fast reflexes:
swift and steady;
deft touch,
on the ball,
acute angles,
you've got it all.
The taste of victory
is within your grasp:
hungry to win;
experience is vast:
you sense your prey
is already beat,
it's just a formality
till you can eat.

French Open – Round 1 (25/5/2010)

Your 1st round match was a tester
but you kept your cool;
you showed the crowd, you're back to rule:
saving breakpoints became your speciality,
they were cheering all around the principality;

a deft touch combined with speed,
power and accuracy gave you the lead;
confident and calm with your fans on your side,
you don't give your opponents an easy ride;
you know how to give them the runaround:
by the end of the match they're homeward bound!

Rafa you rule, you're our 'King of Clay,'
that was another great performance today!

French Open – Round 2 (28/5/2010)

Rafa, I'm so glad you were on first today,
it'll give you more rest before you next play:
when the rain poured down yesterday from Heaven,
I bet you wished it was true, what Toni told you at 7:
he said he was magic and could control the rain,
it's a shame it's not true – he could do it again!

Unfortunately you had to wait till today
for your 2nd round match to get underway,
but as soon as it did, you got stuck in,
racing towards another win.

Courageous and aggressive with power and speed:
other players better take heed,
solid on serve, sharp as a tack,
try as they might, they can't hit back:

when they do the ball goes out,
you're the best, there is no doubt:
lots of topspin makes yours stay in,
you've got the tools for another win;
impressive stuff from our 'King of Clay,'
you've chalked up another win today.

French Open – Round 3 (29/5/2010)

Losing your serve at the start of the match
didn't worry you at all; that's a fact:
you put the pressure back onto Hewitt
and broke right back – the lead, he blew it!

You got the match back on song,
I knew you'd win before too long:
cool and calm, mentally tough,
your tennis told Hewitt, 'That's enough;
I'm in the driving seat, I'm in control,'
you broke him again and moved nearer your goal;
difficult conditions; a windy day,
but you dealt with it well –
you blew us away!

We look in awe at the feats you perform:
amazingly talented, is how you were born.

A competitive match, it was a fight in set 2,
but the decisive break at 4-all went to you;
then you were serving for the 2nd set;
no one's taken one from you yet;
they still haven't; you won it 6-4,
now you're 2 sets up and need one more.

Hewitt's a fighter but you are too,
there wasn't anything he could do,
he stayed competitive, it gave you a test:
but the test proved Rafa – that you're the best:
your relentless pursuit of every point
made sure he was soon outta the joint!

French Open – Round 4 (31/5/2010)

Your match against Belluchi you won in straight sets,
a decisive win; you're a very safe bet;
you've made another piece of history today:
it's your 200th win on that lovely red clay;
98% victories on your favorite surface,
your game's so hot it's like a furnace!

Those victories are even better than Borg's,
as you're still playing, you're collecting hoards:
like last week you became the very first man
to win all 3 clay court masters,
you've shown that you can,
keep piling up the wins and statistics:
but storing the trophies
causes problems with logistics;
but even if your cabinets can't cope any more
it won't stop you adding trophies galore!

French open – Quarter Final (2/6/2010)

The first 3 games, Almagro seized,
it didn't make you very pleased,
so you held serve and then broke back;
determination, you didn't lack;
you held again; now it's 3 all;
back on serve, you showed who rules;
at 6 games all it's tiebreak time,
Rafa, your game was just sublime:
now's the time for drastic measures;
watching you play is such a pleasure;
you won the set after being love 3 in games –
you knew just how to get Almagro tamed.

2nd set, 4 games all; you're break point down:
an amazing point, you hung around:
you hung in there till you won your game;
you weren't letting him take the lead again:
another tiebreak at the end of set 2,
you showed what you're made of,
your talent shone through;
focused, calm and in the zone,
one more set and Almagro's sent home!

The match was close but you still won it in three,
you're as calm and determined as a man can be:
you wrapped it up 6 games to 4;
now you're in the semi-finals once more;
Vamos – you're the boss!

French Open – Semi-Final (4/6/2010)

Your tennis was in top form right from scratch,
you raised your level from the previous match;
you broke Meltzer twice
with your strength and power,
and took the 1st set in about half an hour.

2nd set, you got the break, but then he broke you;
it's just another challenge;
you believed you'd come through,
and come through you did, you broke him again,
you showed him you're in command of the reigns;
that was the set sorted – you won it 6-3;
you'll soon be back at the hotel for tea!

You broke him again at the start of the 3rd,
you're starting to pull away from the herd:
I think your place in the final's reserved!
You're at the top of your game
exhibiting skills and prowess,
it's a joy to watch you,
when you're playing your best;
but when you were serving at 5 games to 3
things suddenly weren't as we want them to be:
love 40 on your serve, you then double fault,
were you feeling a little bit overwrought?
After that you kept your nerve
and held onto your 5-6 serve
to force a tiebreak and win it in three:
it brought a sigh of relief from me!
Every round you've won in straight sets –
and the trophy will be the reward that you'll get.

French Open – Fairy Tale Ending (6/6/10)

Soderling the villain walked onto court first,
then came our hero, to end last year's curse,
to put things right and to win at this final;
his beautiful aura stretches for miles,
shining with goodness, a heart that is gallant,
justice must be done to redress the balance:
like an apple, the trophy must have a bite
by its rightful owner, to make the world right.

Fans' hearts pounding, shallow breathing,
anxious and nervous is how we were feeling,
but you started as you meant to go on,
saved break points on your serve, but on his you won:
you kept your lead and won the 1st set 6-4,
a wonderful start; we couldn't ask for more.

To break in set 2, you were inspired from above,
magnifico tennis as you broke him to love:
wonderful to watch,
you're a champ through and through,
you broke him again and you won it 6-2.

At the start of set 3 you broke his 1st game,
you kept up the intensity
and gave him more of the same,
you can do anything you want with the ball:
like a master class: the Nadal tennis school.

Smart tactics, perfect execution,
to beat you he couldn't find the solution;

your unforced errors were low
and winners were sublime:
you've improved every match
and peaked the right time.

You served for the match at 5 games to 4,
focused and calm, you didn't think of the score;
it all went better than we dared to dream,
you won it to love, you were just supreme.

After the poems I wrote you last year,
it's so wonderful that this year, all of our tears
are tears of joy, not tears of sadness,
you deserved this win
and we're filled with such gladness:

Rafa you played your best tennis
and took out that menace!
Good over evil has triumphed today:
nothing or no one could get in your way,
we're so happy and proud of our 'King of Clay.'

French Open – You Turned Back the Tide

When you went to France we were all on your side,
hoping you'd beat everyone and turn back the tide:
when you're fit it's all yours, you rightfully deserve it;
secretly it's what the other players have to admit.

Even the trophy was homesick, it was tired and fatigued
of living with Federer, he's not in your league! (on clay)

Rafa, you're the French Open Champion 2010,
that trophy is back where it should be again,
back in your arms, where it's most at home,
as long as you're healthy, it won't ever roam.

This year was special; we were all thrilled to witness,
after working so hard to regain your fitness,
you got the reward that you deserved:
now it's the others who are feeling un-nerved.

As your confidence and calm is sky high you know;
with a win like that, it's rightfully so:
you're on top of the world, as high as the sun,
but Rafa, you've always been *my* No.1.

After all your injury problems in 2009,
this year is turning out to be *just* sublime!

Good Luck for Wimbledon 2010

I hope you win Wimbledon, I hope that you can
add another title to your collection of slams;
this year is special after missing last year,
now that you're back, I'll shed happier tears!

You light up the world of those around you,
just by being you,
I hope you win a second time
and make all your dreams come true.

Your blogs always put a smile on my face,
as a tennis player and a man you are just ace,
answering our questions really makes my day,
so much so, I have to say:
thank you Rafa for all you've done,
you'll always be my No.1.

I'm wishing you lots of luck for 2010
and I'll be cheering for you, from my sofa again!

Wimbledon – Round 1 (June 2010)

Rafa, I gasped as I caught the first sight
as you walked onto court in your Wimbledon whites:
clean and tight with muscles beautifully shaped,
I have to say, it was well worth the wait!

Watching you play against Nishikori,
I'm happy to say, it's just the same story
as it was at the French, a straight sets win:
you've shown the others you're a threat again.

Congrats Rafa, a great start you've made,
it was a joy to see the way that you played!

Wimbledon – Round 2 (24/6/2010)

At the start Haase showed he was a very good server
but you kept your calm and didn't let it un-nerve ya,
you weren't intimidated as his aces flew past:
you showed him yours are accurate
and you're built to last.

You played with speed and were very aggressive,
your improvements continued to be progressive:
sure of your ability, calm and serine;
Rafa, you're playing like a dream:
power of shot as you let out an 'ahhh,'
the ball speeds past Haase, his eyes are a blur!

It was a tough match but you kept your cool,
Rafa, you've shown that you're back to rule:
when you kick your leg up and shout 'Vamos,'
you don't let the grass grow,
you show 'em who's boss!

Five sets but a quick match and I wasn't worried,
I knew you'd come through,
your demolition was hurried;
especially in set 4!
You meant business and it showed by your actions:
your attitude so determined and your instant reactions;
you're exciting to watch with your hunger to win,
you've got something special
and it comes from within:
it can't be taught; it's either there or it's not,
but there's no question Rafa –
you've got the lot!

Wimbledon – Round 3 (26/6/2010)

You walk onto court, your cheers are the loudest,
we soak up the atmosphere, as fans we're the proudest;
you settle yourself, make sure everything's right,
and suck your electrolytes so there's no cramps tonight;
you bound to the net where the formalities are done,
then just like a sprinter, to the baseline you run;
after the warm up the umpire says, "play,"
and your round 3 match gets right underway.

You're a beautiful sight when you're in full flow,
come on Rafa, 'Vamos, let's go!'
Such amazing shots, I'm lost for words,
Rafa your tennis is just superb.
You broke his 1st game and won the 1st set,
but Philipp hung in there, he wasn't done yet,
he won the next 2, it got really tight,
but you weren't giving up, you were ready to fight;
it was another 5 setter for our spectacular Spaniard,
your will to win was the highest standard,
even though it wasn't easy for you
with shoulder and knee problems and a warning too!

Why you were warned I haven't a clue,
that umpire doesn't know you the way that we do,
you're as trustworthy and honest as the day is long,
you wouldn't have coaching, that umpire was wrong!

Your fans are so happy you came through today,
we're eagerly waiting for your 4th round display
of speed and dexterity, power and touch,
we love watching you Rafa, so very much!

Wimbledon – Round 4 (28/6/2010)

Rafa I'm so happy that your knee was fine today,
and that you had an easier win,
with two sets less to play;
so you can have more rest
and your knee will be much fresher:
and then when you play Soderling,
it won't be under pressure.
Today you were efficient,
you won like you wanted to,
without any pain or problems,
that's what we want for you:
we want you to be happy,
we want you to be fit;
we want you to win Wimbledon –
then the sky's the limit.
You said that after Wimbledon,
you're getting treatment on your knee,
so it's as perfect as the other one –
it'll match your perfect body!
Your fans are all excited
with more great wins to come,
and we'll all be supporting you
as we've always done;
so we're feeling optimistic,
you're having a great year,
and we know it will continue
as your talent's very clear,
and you're managing your fitness
much better than before,
the result of that is lots more wins,
of that you are assured.

Wimbledon Quarter Final – 30/6/2010

Against Soderling, the 1st set made us worry and frown,
at one point you were actually love 5 down,
but you broke him back to lose it 3-6,
you then came alive and your problems were fixed.

2nd set you broke him and won it 6-3,
it was 'Vintage Nadal' and we love what we see,
3rd set you broke again and were serving 5-4,
but he called the trainer –
the wait was 8 minutes or more!

Your body cooled down and you lost your serve,
he leveled the match but you held your nerve,
it went to a tiebreak, we're so glad you won,
that set was yours Rafa – justice was done!

Things keep on happening that seem so unfair,
umpires need more training, they should be more aware,
but Rafa you didn't let it affect you,
justice and good prevailed, it's true!

By the 4th set you were on a roll,
nothing could stop you reaching your goal,
your place in the semi has now been booked,
I'm sure you won't let Murray off the hook!

Wimbledon Semi Final – 2/7/2010

You said since you last played him
your confidence is higher,
it certainly showed, your game was on fire!
We knew you meant business
with your aggressive play,
Murray didn't know what hit him today!
Quick out of the blocks, you didn't hang about;
your fans are so happy, 'Vamos,' we did shout;
you won the 1st set with just 1 unforced error,
you showed Murray
beating you would be a tough endeavour;
the 2nd set went to a tiebreak
and you made sure you won,
an impressive scoreboard, two sets to none;
then you lost your serve at the start of set three,
suddenly a glimmer of hope for Murray –
I knew you'd still win, you broke back at 3-4,
a true champion, you took command once more:
you won the next two games and took it in three;
your hunger to win was plain to see,
like a bull tossing his prey high in the air,
you stayed calm on important points:
courageously you dare,
'he who dares wins,' is what they say,
Rafa we're thrilled that you dared today!
Another final awaits you on Sunday,
I'm sure you'll be hugging the trophy by Monday;
I've said this before but I'll say it again,
I think it's so true, it really is plain:
if the amount of fans affects the outcome,
then Rafa, you'll be the winning one!

Wimbledon Final – 4/7/2010

On the long walk from the locker room,
you bounced along ready for a fight,
as you followed Berdych onto court,
the crowd all came alight.

He served 1st so you were always one game behind,
but at 3 games all, inspiration you did find,
then you held serve and broke him a second time
to take it 6-3, with tennis sublime.

You served first at the start of set 2,
it lasted 10 minutes but you came through,
it was close, till he was serving to stay alive,
but you broke him then, and won the set 7-5.

The 3rd set was a similar tale,
you were patient and knew that you wouldn't fail,
when he served at 4-5 you upped your game,
you broke him right there and won Wimby again!

You had explosive energy from start to finish,
and you won it in three, his game you diminished,
you fell to the ground, you've done it again,
we're all so happy you're back to reign.

Rafa Wins Our Hearts All Over Again

Centre court is special, full of history and tradition,
once a young Spanish boy had a dream and a vision:
to win at Wimbledon would be a dream come true,
now he's not just won it once, today he's made it two!

Rafael Nadal is the man
we've taken to our hearts with glee,
he's the most talented, humble and thoughtful player
we've had the privilege to see:
watching his speech, we're all so proud,
Rafa's so loved by the Wimbledon crowd,
we're thrilled that he said he loves it here too,
if we could adopt him, we really would do!

He took his trophy to the Wimby front door,
to pose for pictures and see fans galore:
he signed autographs and high fived his fans,
we can't help loving him, he's a wonderful man.

U.S. Open 2010 – Career Grand Slam

The career Grand Slam and you're just 24,
9 slams so far and I know you'll win more;
you're making history as your career advances,
you make the most of all your chances.

You won Monte Carlo 6 years in a row;
an amazing feat and your rivals all know;
then Rome, Madrid and the French once more –
no one's ever done that before!

You're on a roll on the crest of a wave,
3 slams this year, the route you did pave;
after your injuries you did all you could
to get back to your best; we knew that you would.

Now you've surpassed what your best used to be,
you've excelled even more now you're injury free;
you deserve it so much; you're a real inspiration;
you teach by example, showing such dedication;
so many of us want to be just like you,
not only in tennis but in our lives too.

He Hasn't Put a Foot Wrong

Rafa's like a winning machine
with style and finesse like you've never seen;

superior shots, stunning to watch;
his talent makes the opponent botch:

high over the net with a lot of pace
allows a margin for error that makes his game ace;

the world's best was at his best,
his forehand was lethal and so was the rest!

Savage beauty, aggressive and purposeful,
he's got every shot in the book as a tool:

poetry in motion, cliché but true –
I think that even the opponent knew.

Vamos – Lets Make It 7 in a Row! (2011)

You're through to the semis,
I hope you do well,
I'm rooting for you,
I think you can tell!
Come on Rafa,
'Vamos,' let's go,
I'm sure you can make it
7 in a row!
With talent like yours
I have no doubt,
round by round
you'll knock 'em all out,
so you'll be standing
there alone,
biting the trophy
while they all go home!

Rafa's 7th Heaven (Monte Carlo 2011)

Monte Carlo or bust is what they say
but you just 'bust' another record today,
you've been champion 7 years in a row,
your 7th Heaven is Monte Carlo!

An amazing feat by an amazing player,
you ran round the court like a dragon slayer;
I'm so very proud of what you've done,
I'm a one man woman and you're my number 1.

I hope this gives your confidence a boost,
so you can play your top level
and cut the nerves loose;
I hope it's the start of another winning run,
now the clay court season has just begun;

then when it's time to move onto grass,
you'll continue your run with mucho class!

6 Time French Open Champion (2011)

You're the French Open Champ Rafa, now 6 times,
the journey to get there was a difficult climb,
but you focused and fought each step of the way:
you hung in there when your game went astray;

then you found your best tennis at just the right time,
'Vintage Nadal,' your game was sublime,
and you've equalled Borg's record
of 6 wins at the French,
I think you'll surpass it
and more wins you will clench.

The way that you did it you've gained even more
respect and admiration than you had before,
and before you had lots, but it's now overflowing,
you wore your heart on your sleeve
and my love keeps on growing.

I admire what you've done
and the way that you've done it,
you showed great determination and loads of true grit;
so I send congrats to you, my favourite player,
you're more heroic to me than a big dragon slayer!

Rafa v Murray (Wimbledon Semi 1/7/2011)

Rafa, only 7 unforced errors you made,
your tennis is hot
and you're really our fave,
I bet you're not the opponents fave though,
cos when they play you,
it's homeward they go!

With anesthetic in your foot,
numbing the pain,
you fought like a warrior
and beat Andy again.

After losing the 1st set
you stepped up a gear,
even when you fell,
you amazed the fans here:
your racket flew up
as you fell down,
but you caught it in one hand
from your place on the ground!

Everything you did
was thrilling to see,
I hope you win the final
when it's on my TV.

Rafa's Raring to Go!

You're eating so healthy,
you'll have lots of energy,
so when you go onto court,
you'll beat all your arch enemies,
not literally –
I know that you're friendly with rivals,
but that doesn't mean
your game will be stifled,
side to side
you'll make 'em run all over the place,
then you'll hit a great pass
right into the space;
the commentator remarks,
"Oh I say what a pass,
it's the best we've seen on the Wimbledon grass!"
You're confident, calm
and have complete control,
focused and sure
that you'll reach your goal:
major number eleven,
Wimbledon trophy number three,
you biting the trophy –
I'm sure we will see.
(Unfortunately, so far,
he's not made it to three!)

Toronto – In the Pink

You wore a bright pink top; I like it a lot;
it suits you and your game –
both are exciting and hot!

As per usual, your aim in Toronto
was not only to win but to wrap it up pronto;
your 1st set back on hard courts was close and long:
it wasn't pronto but your confidence grew strong.

After toweling off, a few skips to the baseline,
body language confident – it's tiebreak time;
saving set points, it was as close as it could get,
but you played with calm and won the 1st set.

Then in the 2nd set you got into your stride,
you kept your focus and had an easier ride:
no need for a tiebreak as you broke his serve;
every match to you is a learning curve.

You aim to improve each time you play,
that's why you're so successful today,
and your rivals all know that whatever they do,
you'll never give up – that's just not you.

Paris Masters (Round Two)

At 2–3 your service game went all wrong,
it cost you the set, but before very long,
you got back to business and turned it around,
so you were the one back in command.

1st Service, 2nd Set, you hung on for dear life,
you seemed to be in a whole heap of strife,
you pulled through after 8 minutes or so;
but lost your next serve, oh no, oh no!

You broke back real quick, then took the lead,
you have 'true grit' in times of need:
you hung in there and took the 2nd set,
you told Almagro, "I'm not done yet;"
but not before giving us a rollercoaster ride,
guts and determination is what you applied.

The Final Set was just as nail-biting,
but as always, you kept on fighting:
you got broken, then broke back,
excitement is something your match didn't lack;
always playing catch up and it wasn't much fun,
like a cat with 9 lives and you used every one!

I was worried that something was wrong with you,
but you hung in there and you pulled through:
It seemed a struggle for you today,
I hope it feels easier next time you play.
Oh Rafa, you gave us such a big fright,
but we're all so thrilled that you won tonight!

Aussie Semi 2012 – Rafa Wraps It up in 4

I wasn't worried when you were 1-4 down,
I knew you'd be able to turn it around:
even losing the 1st set,
you clung on like a vine,
you don't play the scoreboard,
it's one point at a time.

You know what to do to get Roger rattled,
you've won 19 of your umpteen battles:
the stats speak for themselves –
your tennis does the talking:
now out of the tournament,
Roger is walking!

Your level of tennis is high:
your shots are magnifico,
when the final day dawns
you'll be raring to go;
another great chance to add to your slams,
I think that the trophy will be in your hands!

Rafa's 9th Wonder (French Open 2014)

On the edge of my seat,
heart in mouth:
watching the final,
my stomach drops south;
when he lost the 1st set
I was worried for Rafa,
but he won set 2
and showed he's still the gaffer!
Such a close match:
glued to the screen,
whole body tense
then 'Vamos' I scream!
Rafa won set 3 as well,
he had control of the match
but in set 4, I was worried
that Novak would then snatch.
When Rafa bent in the fourth,
I thought his back was sore,
I didn't want Novak
to take control once more;
but Rafa did what Rafa does best:
he stayed strong and focused
and his talent did the rest;
his 9th French Open
he won it in four,
now 14 major titles
and he's coming back for more!

Rafa v Rosol (Round 2 Wimbledon 2014)

Two years ago, Rosol beat Rafa in five;
he cheated with distractions
and mind games, so sly:
but this year Rafa was ready for him,
there's no way he'd let him distract him again.
Today we were worried, a set and a break down,
but Rafa still aimed to kick him right outta town;
he didn't want history to repeat itself:
he wanted a chance to put that trophy
right back on his shelf:
he pumped himself up, rallied and ran,
he believed in himself
and got the best of that man –
now he's defended his points
and he's into round 3,
he won't give a point away
to anyone for free;
it's all gains from here,
increasing his lead
as the world No.1,
he deserves it – indeed!
They say revenge is a dish best served cold,
but Rafa got it cos his tennis was hot,
he wasn't gonna let Rosol get the better of him,
so he gave him as good as he got!
'Vamos' Rafa!
You've showed 'em you've still got it,
you can beat anyone if you're healthy and fit.

Rafa's Go Faster Stripes

His go faster stripes are working again,
after his 2nd match when he was in pain;

but today he seemed confident, healthy and fit,
Rafa strides forward, Nadal never quits;

the more rounds he plays the better he gets;
the odds are dropping on those outside bets;

he's a real contender for that Aussie title –
another opponent bites the dust
and says 'Good night all.'

Stuttgart 2015

6-4, 6-3, 6-1,
into view the real Rafa has come:
he places the ball
with surgical precision,
Rafa Nadal is a man on a mission;
people keep saying
he's not the Rafa of old,
our hero will show he is;
consider them told!

He served aces on break points
and hung onto his serve:
he showed the critics
he can still hold his nerve;
he played a great match,
now round 2's under his belt;
he played a real blinder –
the knockout's been dealt!

The racket shaped trophy,
he went on to win:
the 1st on grass,
in 5 years for him.

Reach For The Stars

Reach for the stars Rafa,
set your goals high,
I admire your positive attitude
of 'never say die.'
I'm English,
so Wimbledon is my favourite slam,
and I want you to win it –
you're my favourite man!

Pre Match (Round 2 Wimbledon 2/7/15)

Brown is a tough one,
he beat you once before;
but if we can help it,
he won't anymore!
You feel at home here,
we'll be on your side,
so getting that win
might be an easier ride;
with us Brits all cheering loudly for you
helping to make
your Wimbledon dreams all come true.

The Rafa Mentality (2/8/15)

A hungry look in his eyes,
walking with purposeful strides,
never give up, never say die,
'The Rafa mentality' you just can't buy;
he makes every moment count
from the 1st point to the last,
like his life depends on winning that point –
he won't let his chances pass;
he hangs in there, makes them play another ball,
while he stays strong and he watches them fall,
hungry, eager, ready to pounce,
he hits a smash so hard, it does a ten foot bounce;
psyched and focused, in the zone,
determined to be the winner when he goes home.
(and he was)

The Real Rafa is Back (2/8/15)

The real Rafa is back!
His previous losses don't mean Jack!
He played with more belief than we've seen in a while
and with that came his winning smile.

If I get cramp
it hurts so much I always end up swearing;
but even cramp couldn't take away
the smile that he was wearing!

We'll remember this milestone,
he made sure things went his way,
he made sure Fogninni was the loser today!

It was a hard fought match
but Rafa won in straight sets;
it's a match Fogninni will try to forget!

Rafa was relentless, he never gave up,
now he's the winner with that clover shaped cup!
Vamos, you're the boss!

Rafa v Coric (Round 1 U.S. Open 2015)

Rafa's in black with pink 'go faster' stripes,
and Coric didn't live up to the hype;

just cos he beat Rafa on their 1st meeting;
this time Rafa was doing the beating!

Coric wouldn't give up: like a dog with a bone,
he won set 3, but Rafa still sent him home!

Rafa v Shwartzman (R2 U.S. Open 2015)

Illuminous and dark green for the day wear,
his own light, he has brought;
if the match goes on until dark,
his clothes'll light up the court!

He won round 2 in three,
but I feared that wouldn't be,
4-1 up but the opponent fought back,
Rafa won the tiebreak to get back on track.

Set 2 Rafa lost his serve,
but our champ fought back again;
he won the set, now he's 2 sets up,
one more he needs to gain.

Shwartzman didn't make it easy:
set 3 was still hard fought,
but Rafa pulled through 7-5,
then his smile lit up the court!
(as well as his clothes).

China Round 1 (Beijing 2015)

Confidence growing,
good feelings are flowing,
into the groove
with lots of good moves:
a good days play,
back to winning ways;
Rafa's on his way there,
he's come well prepared,
gaining points every round,
the opponent's home bound!
A close match with lots of breaks,
but Rafa showed he's got what it takes!
Vamos Champ –
I'm in your camp!

Nadal v Pospisol (Round 2 Beijing 7/10/15)

Serving consistently, Rafa didn't get broken,
watch out opponents, his tennis has spoken;
his tennis did the talking and I'm happy to say,
Rafa notched up another great win today.

A close scoreboard, it all went with serve,
till tie break time, Rafa held his nerve:
he won the 1st set with tennis phenomenal,
he makes the opponent look abominable!

2nd set Rafa broke to lead at 3-2,
then won his serve to consolidate it too,
tennis so hot, it was just blazing –
Rafa was playing absolutely amazing!

Nadal v Sock (Quarter Final Beijing 9/10/15)

On a quarter of the court, the sun was still out,
it would've been hard to see the ball;
of that there's no doubt;
Rafa served 1st and won it with ease,
but next time round
he lost his serve, and Sock was pleased;
he saved break points on his next serve
to avoid going a double break down,
he worked real hard but couldn't break back
when Socks next serve came around;
he lost set 1, 6 games to 3,
but in set 2, came the reprise:
he broke Socks serve at the start of the set,
Rafa fans knew he wasn't beat yet,
he upped his game to win it 6-4,
now it's the deciding set once more.
A fight in the crowd disrupted the start,
the umpire called security to pull them apart!
Vintage Nadal came out to seize control of the set;
he broke at 4-3, now he looks a sure bet;
playing a high level, he broke again to win,
I always had complete faith in him.
I'm glad Sock didn't pull up his socks,
cos today, only Rafa's game rocks!

Fogninni v Rafa (Semi Final Beijing 2015)

1st set, Fogninni broke you,
but you broke him back too,
I think this match has a little de ja vu;
you held serve 1st and led it 2-1,
then broke him again, 3-1 is more fun!

Fabio broke back on your next serve,
now this de ja vu's getting on my nerves;
I only like de ja vu when it's in Rafa's favour,
they're the de ja vu's I always savour;
you both held serve till you lead 6-5,
you broke him then and his 1st set hopes all died!

2nd set went with serve till he served at 2-3,
you broke him right there,
so in the lead you would be,
seriously fired up you won your next serve to love,
leading 5-2, you show him who's guv,
you had 2 match points on his serve,
but he held, now you're 5-3,
you serve it out and win, it just HAD to be!

Fogninni reminds me of Freddie Mercury,
well he was another one to bite the dust,
you've shown you're in complete control,
and now you've got it sussed!

Vamos champ,
I'm always in your camp!

Karlovic v Nadal (Round 2 Shanghai 2015)

You lost your 1st serve, playing catch-up from the start,
but with character like yours, you didn't lose heart;
you hung in there and kept it close,
you went up a gear and gave him a dose
of Vintage Nadal, you broke right back,
you won the set 7-5, you're right on track.

2nd set you serve 1st, you hold this time,
confidence is higher, you're feeling fine,
you had a few deuce's on your serve at 2 all:
but you come through in the end with a winning ball,
love 40 at 4 all, you gave us a scare,
but you bounced back to win,
with tennis beyond compare;
it goes to a tiebreak but he wins it,
but that still doesn't dampen your spirit.

The deciding set goes with serve, it's scary for us fans,
but we know with you, Rafa, it's in safe hands,
you're getting back to your very best
and in this match you passed the test;
you held serve at 4-5 to stay in the match
and again at 5-6, it's a purple patch!
Another tiebreak to decide it all
but you're a genius with a tennis ball;
you held on tight till you broke his serve,
he was the one that lost his nerve,
you won with style, with character and heart,
in Shanghai, you've made an amazing start.

Rafa beat Raonic (Round 3 Shanghai 2015)

Rafa's got his mojo back,
Confidence, he no longer lacks;

that look of eager determination,
knowing whoever it is, he could face 'em,

like he knows inside that he can win,
his aura's come back from wherever it's been,

a straight sets win 6-3,7-6,
everything that was wrong, Rafa has fixed;

and his millions of fans are all so delighted,
and in his happiness, we're all united!

Rafa v Warwinka (Quarters Shanghai 15)

It's all about what's between his ears,
now Rafa's got rid of all his fears;

oozing confidence from every pore,
on Warwinka's hopes, he slammed the door;

his faithful fans waited for this resurrection
as he skillfully hits in any direction;

he's always had the talent, it was just a mental block,
but now he's found the key to the lock;

his highest level of tennis has come to the fore,
and the Real Rafa is here once more!

It's like an alien took Rafa and left his double to play;
I'm thrilled that the real Rafa is back today!

Rafa v Rosol (Basel 26/10/15)

1-6, 4-5, 0-30 down,
but don't count Rafa out,
do so at your peril,
he's a fighter; don't ever doubt!
You could see in his face,
he was there every point,
aiming to kick Rosel right outta the joint!
There's history between them,
there's no love lost there:
Rosel started his unsportsmanlike antics,
as usual his antics weren't fair;
but Rafa had a determined demeanor,
he took it all in his stride,
the crowd didn't like Rosel's antics,
they made it clear they were on Rafa's side.
Rafa caught up from behind in set 2
and in the tiebreak in set 3,
he was positive, determined and calm,
I think that was the key;
the real Rafa is back,
he's put the nerves to bed;
now he's got into the groove,
there'll be more wins ahead.

Rafa v Rosol (Basel 26/10/15)

2 Points from defeat,
but Rafa clawed his way back to win,
his fans nerves are frayed,
we all need tonic and gin!
Actually I don't drink,
I only wrote that cos it rhymes,
now the real Rafa is back,
and that's another of the signs.
I'm all hyped up with happiness,
I can't wind down tonight,
so I thought I'd write another poem
about Rafa's amazing fight!
Rafa said it was a hard match to get into,
but he hung in there and waited for his chance,
I was so thrilled that he managed to win,
I did a vamossing dance!

Rafa v Dimitrov (Basel 28/10/15)

Rafa's an expert at winning from a losing position,
being down in the score doesn't alter his mission;
the false sense of security he gives them,
and his determined power of will,
is all that he needs to go in for the kill:
and kill it he does, with forehands down the line,
and volleys and smashes,
they're in every time;
now he's warmed up, they don't stand a chance,
soon he'll be doing his vamossing dance!
Dimitrov suffered the same fate as Rosol:
they started off winning,
so their loss was colossal!

Rafa v Cilic (Basel 30/10/15)

1st set, non-descript, going with serve,
but I thought you were still a sure bet;
until Cilic broke you, and from under your nose
he stole the bloomin' set!

Line calls, challenges, Hawkeye you didn't believe;
you spoke to the umpire, you were really quite peeved;
you lost your serve at the start of set 2,
but being a set and a break down didn't phase you;
you broke him back and broke again,
you won the set with your competitive brain.

You broke him at the start of the 3rd,
you mounted your attack;
it's exciting to see you win from behind,
Rafa, your 'aura' is back.

4-6, 6-3, 6-3, the other players will see,
it doesn't matter if you're close to defeat;
you'll find a way to turn up the heat!

Rafa v Rosol (Paris 4/11/15)

He's a tricky one:
playing Rosol's not much fun;
but Rafa stayed in the zone
and sent Rosol right on home.

A comprehensive victory of 6-2, 6-2,
there was simply nothing Rosol could do:
Rafa played closer to the baseline,
he took away Rosol's time,
hitting some fantastic angles;
his winners were sublime.

The last couple of months his confidence has grown
and he's sending more of the others home!

World Tour Finals 2015 (1st Match)

World Tour Finals start on Sunday,
Rafa plays 8pm on Monday;
he plays Warwinka and last time he lost:
but I think on Monday he'll win, whatever the cost;
hopefully no blood, but sweat and tears,
will help him win, as he moves through the gears,
I'm sure the crowd will be on his side,
Rafa's performances fill us with pride.

He won in straight sets –
that match we won't forget;
it was a really good start,
he played with passion and heart.

World Tour Finals 2015 (2nd Match)

Rafa's 2nd match was Murray,
I thought it'd be tough but I needn't have worried;

Rafa came through with flying colours,
now, in the round robin he's ahead of the others;

for the semi-final he has qualified,
Rafa fans are beaming with pride;

on Saturday he faces Novak,
I'm hoping Rafa will tame him back

and get to the final to give himself a chance
to add the World Tour Finals –
and his CV he'll enhance.

World Tour Finals 2015 (3rd Match)

Ferrer was a tough one,
he won the 1st set,

but you wanted three out of three wins,
it wasn't over yet;

but now you've got your confidence back,
it helped you to pull through,

it was an entertaining match,
with Ferrer as determined as you:

it must be something in the Spanish water,
Spaniards are such a determined crew!

you won the next 2 sets, 6-3, 6-3,
even in a dead rubber, your best, you had to be.

Rafa – Our Prize Fighter

You have an aura of invincibility
that you wear like a cloak:
your opponent's psyched out,
he's ready to choke.

You jump and bounce at the start of the match,
another win, from his grasp, you aim to snatch;
then to the baseline you sprint with vigour,
your physique looks powerful; stronger and bigger.

In the opponent's mind you're all over the place;
you're the one he didn't want to face;
in your mind you always have the assurance
that you can beat them all, with skill and endurance.

Like a prize fighter you deliver – you hit so well;
but your opponent won't be saved by the bell:
you stay on his case till you knock him out;
you make sure of it – you have no doubt.

Chapter Two – Less Losses Luckily!

This chapter is about some of Rafa's losses and how it makes us fans feel – luckily during Rafa's career he has had less losses than wins and has an amazing record of 14 Grand Slams and 27 Masters 1000 titles so far.

World Tour Finals Loss 2009

Rafa you can hold your head up high:
no one can say you didn't try;
you gave it everything you've got,
at times your tennis was red hot!

Seeing you try so hard but not break through,
I felt your pain; I felt it too;
losing confidence and feeling frustration
made it hard to relax and get good sensations;
but you tried so hard, you were persistent,
then your tennis was more consistent:
in the 2nd set you got it together,
Rafa you're getting better and better;
I for one was so impressed,
soon Rafa, you'll be at your best!

Semi-Final Loss to Ljubachic (March 2010)

At first you seemed confident,
it went according to plan,
but right near the end, it all went down the pan;
it didn't go exactly according to your script:
you lost opportunities, then your level dipped –
but you still got further than No.'s 1 and 2:
you'll soon sort it out; I have faith in you.

In your artillery you have the ammunition
to beat all the others and complete your mission;
when you're the last man standing,
it'll begin a winning run
and this 'almost made it but not quite,'
will soon be over and done.

You'll soon be winning all the time,
and after having problems it'll be sublime:
it'll mean so much more; you'll feel so great,
it'll be *so* well worth the wait!

Loss to Roddick (Semi Final Miami 2010)

Rafa, in my eyes you're such a great champion;
when you win you show the loser such kind compassion,
and you're one who takes losses
with courteous good will:
a wonderful asset that you have instilled.

You're one who uses setbacks as a motivational aid
to come back stronger, not wither and fade;
one who's determined and never stops trying:
he has an inner knowing that soon he'll be flying,
on the crest of a wave, as high as a kite;
it's a case of 'I will win,' not a case of 'I might.'

Self-talk is very important for you:
you've used it to win many titles, it's true;
the adversity you faced will make you stronger,
so when you reach the top, you'll stay there longer;
this is something I'm sure is true,
Rafa I have complete faith in you.

I'm sure a trophy is within your sights,
believe in yourself and you'll reach great heights:
this is something I've learnt from you –
that's why I know, you believe it too!

Rafa's on Fire

Rafa was on fire today,
he's getting in the groove,
his opponents better watch out,
he's got a thing or two to prove!

He's a man on a mission,
he'll show them all who's boss:
he's got extra motivation
after the Barcelona loss.

Red hot Rafa
forehand on the run,
no better sight in tennis –
except perhaps his bum!

Miami Final (2014)

Rafa your fans feel so sad for you
but so proud you tried till the match was through;

we know how you feel, it wasn't much fun,
but you did your best, that's all you could've done;

it came as a shock, Novak's tactics had changed:
there just wasn't time for yours to re-arrange;

in a best of three sets, time goes so fast,
over five sets his purple patch wouldn't last;

now you can analyse how he managed that feat
and work out the solution for when you next meet;

but don't worry Rafa, we'll always be here
cheering for you – so don't ever fear;

keep your spirits up, don't feel dejected,
win or lose, you'll always be respected –
next time your winning game will be resurrected!

Rafa's Wimbledon 4th Round Loss (2014)

This man has character,
I love this man,
this man works so hard,
have you guessed I'm a fan?
If he ever fails to achieve his aim,
he'll be back next time to try again.
What could he do?
No more could he have done:
seeing aces fly past you,
isn't much fun,
but this man's work ethic
is second to none;
he'll keep trying and achieving
as long as he's breathing!
I admire him just as much after a loss:
he'll re-group and bounce back,
and show them who's boss!

Sad Loss

We share your sadness
at losing today,
it's human and normal
to feel that way,
especially after having
wins all the time,
it feels very strange,
like a difficult climb.
It's as hard for us watching
as it is for you,
we want you to win
as much as you do;
remember you're the winner
that you were before,
that winner's inside you,
he'll emerge lots more.
Things will get better,
how could they not,
with the work ethic
and the talent you've got;
you're getting much closer
to the winner inside,
he'll come back soon
and you'll have an easier ride.
Don't be disheartened,
believe in yourself –
you'll soon win more trophies
to put on your shelf!

French Loss and Luck for Queens (2015)

When you lost at the French I shed a tear
but I'm sure you'll be back to win it next year;

you took it so well
you're quite a philosopher,
your mum brought you up well,
it must be because of her!

Good luck at Queens Rafa, I hope you do well,
I'm cheering for you, I think you can tell;
you have millions of fans, all very keen
to see you biting that great big trophy at Queens.

Wimbledon Exit Round 2 (2015)

Everything is temporary,
that's the way life goes:
winning streaks can't last forever,
his opponents better be on their toes –

Rafa's losing ways can't continue,
his bad patch will soon be ending;
that's an unwritten rule of the Universe,
so lots more wins are pending.

Rafa's time will come again,
his recent conquerors better watch out:
the day will come when he'll beat them all
of that I have no doubt!

Next Time

Next time it'll be a different story,
Rafa will hang tough to claim the glory;
he showed what he's made of, he wouldn't give up:
he wanted a chance to win that Montreal Cup;
if it had been 5 sets
he'd have had more time to work it out –
I know he will, I have no doubt;
Nishikori's joy won't be long lasting
cos Rafa's game plan, he'll be enhancing,
and next time they meet, he'll win for sure,
he won't beat Rafa anymore!
It won't be plain sailing
but things that are worth it, never are:
when he gets there he'll have come so far,
and then it'll mean more than ever
and Nishikori will hit stormy weather!

Nadal v Tsonga – China Semi (4-6, 6-0, 5-7)

Tsonga beat Nadal, but not according to the score;
it should've been Tsonga, kicked out that door,
but out of the tournament Rafa did go;
when he'd won 2 more games than Jo!

It's very frustrating for Rafa fans
but the scoring system is out of our hands!
It doesn't often happen,
but when it does I'm saddened;
to win more games but lose the match;
it's a tennis system scoring catch!

The final set was close,
it could've gone either way,
and Rafa still looked at the positives today;
as a fan I see them too:
more wins ahead for Rafa, it's true!

In my eyes Rafa's still the winner,
it's a tennis scoring system sinner!

Federer v Nadal (Basel Final 01/11/15)

You lost set 1 with just one loss of serve:
but you clinched set 2, you held your nerve,
the final set you didn't manage;
but this loss, to your confidence will not damage,
as your improving daily and getting nearer
to your very best form, it couldn't be clearer;
soon all your rivals will once again fear ya!

"Thanks for your support all week,"
you said to the crowd,
but their cheers for Federer today,
were much more loud;
you said "Today was a little less but I understand,"
(because he was in Federer's home land)
he said it with that gorgeous smile,
the crowd showed their love for quite a while.

U.S. Open Rollercoaster Round 3 (2015)

Set 1 you broke 1st but then he broke back,
but it didn't stop you from staying on track;
you broke him again and won it 6-3,
you're into the groove, I like what I see;
unforced errors were low so confidence is growing,
I'm liking the way that this match is going.

2nd Set, 4 all, his serve, deuce,
you got the break; he gave his racket abuse!
Serving for the set, your 40 love turned to deuce,
but giving up is something that you refuse;
an amazing point, you hung in there well,
till Fogninni put it out
and 'vamos' you did yell.

Set 3, like set 1, you lost the break you had,
serving at 4-5 it all went bad,
Fogninni won the set when your ball went out,
stay strong Rafa, don't have doubts.

4th Set you broke him then he broke back,
excitement is something the match didn't lack,
but he broke you again to go to 5-3,
now I've got butterflies in my tummy!
Come on Rafa – break back now
you can do it – show him how!
But he didn't and Fogninni won it 6-3;
now a 5 setter, it has to be.

5th Set, you served 1st and held to love,
he did the same, no one is the guv;

but you lost your next serve, down 1-2,
you broke back right away,
you knew what to do:
2 all, your serve, love 40 down,
you got to 30-40 but couldn't hang around,
Fogninni breaks again and leads 3-2;
but you broke back again – you just had to!

3 games all, final set, you lose serve again, down 3-4,
my stomach's in knots, can't take much more!
You fight and fight from 0-40 down
deuce after deuce, you hung around,
you broke back, 4 all, but there's a catch –
you lost your next serve so he's serving for the match.
He wins 6-4, your ball went out,
but Rafa, you'll win again, I have no doubt!

It broke my heart to see you sad,
walking back, carrying your bags,
gutted is how you look, and how I feel,
you'll always be the player with the most appeal,
you tug my heartstrings, I love you so,
I'm so sad to see you go.

Positive Vibes for Rafa

Believe in your heart that Rafa will win,
start sending good vibes today,
so tomorrow when he faces Novak,
he'll play his top level of play.

Pray tonight to help him to
stay calm and fit and well,
so tomorrow when he walks on court,
everything will jell.
If millions of fans do it,
we'll help affect the outcome,
and as sure as eggs are eggs,
Rafa'll be the winning one.

Novak beat Nadal (Beijing Final 11/10/15)

The match was closer than the scoreboard showed;
Rafa's getting closer to the Rafa of old,

it's a process to get there, and get there he will;
he's positive and motivated as he climbs up that hill,

he got to the final, that's no mean feat,
and Novak's the only one he couldn't beat:

that's nothing to be ashamed of,
Novak's playing like a demon,

but Rafa'll get his revenge,
sometime next season!

Pandemonium in Paris

The days play started at 13 hundred hours
but you weren't on till 23 hundred,
I think that was just ridiculous,
cos at that time the body clock plundered.

You had a good start and were 2-0 up
but serving for the set he broke back,
it went to a tie break and he won through,
but determination you didn't lack.

The tournament turned up the heating:
remember, it's an indoor court;
dripping with sweat, Rafa said he was too hot,
more problems, the heating brought.

Stan wanted a coffee due to a headache,
a white cup appeared by his chair,
but caffeine is a stimulant,
I don't think that was fair!

The 2nd set went to a tiebreak
and he won that as well;
it was 1.15 in the morning:
that was the end of the match from hell!

I don't think it'll damage Rafa's confidence,
it was close, and he'll win next time,
and I'm sending my poem to sky TV,
to give them a piece of my mind!

I hope they tell the tournament

their scheduling is very unfair
and their heat torture could make the players faint,
but it seems that they don't care!

As for letting Stan drink coffee,
and giving him the edge,
the tournament and umpires should all be fairer,
they need to take a pledge!

World Tour Finals 2015 (Semi-Final)

Djokovic was your biggest challenge;
in the Semi's, you faced him,
he beat you with just one break in each set;
you couldn't get the win.

Less than a dozen unforced errors for you,
he had over double, but he had more winners too:
the way that he was playing,
there was nothing you could do,

but you'll analyse it and work out a game plan
so next time you meet,
you'll be the winning man.

Rafa v Verdasco (Aussie Open 2016)

Last time in 2009 you were on a winning streak,
but in 2016 you were getting back on your feet;
last time you won in 5 sets
and it went to 5 sets again,
but sadly for us Rafa fans
the outcome wasn't the same.

Last time you met him in the semi-final,
but this year it was a tough 1st round;
and he was hitting bombs in the final set
so it was you, that was homeward bound.

We had high hopes for you in Oz,
but now my heart goes out because
I feel for you, when things don't go your way,
I want you to win every time you play;
I know it's not realistic to win all the time,
and getting back to your best is a difficult climb,
I hope that soon you'll work things out;
I'll always be in your camp,
without a doubt!

Hard Losses

It must be so hard for Rafa,
going through all this in the public eye;
especially when some people are saying
it's the start of his demise;
they're saying he's past his best,
or worse still that he's finished:
but there's nothing they can say to me,
that'll make my faith diminish:
a diehard fan of Rafa,
is what I'll always be,
I'll stay loyal to only him,
he's the one for me!
He's the one that's loved the most,
he's the most exciting player to see,
the one that's respected beyond compare;
his true fans will not flee!
As long as he's around,
we'll all be there too,
supporting him forever,
we're the Rafa supporting crew!

Less Losses Luckily

Each time Rafa loses,
as a fan my heart does sink,
but his career's had less losses luckily:
he's not often on the brink!

If he loses he gets more determined
to improve his tennis and tactics,
sometimes a small alteration
will make an improvement that's really dramatic.

He's working on playing closer to the baseline,
and on being more aggressive,
these changes are reaping rewards,
and his improvement is progressive.

There're less losses to write about
and for that I'm very glad;
27 Masters 1000's and 14 Grand Slams and counting,
isn't a passing fad!

Chapter Three – Injury Time Out

Rafa has had problems with his knees, stomach tears and an appendicitis which he continued to play through and this chapter is about his injury time out and how us fans feel during these times.

Dandelion Wishes

I made a wish on this dandelion seed,
I hope it helps you to succeed,
I hope it's just as lucky for you
as the one in Australia you wished on too.
I hope that history repeats itself
and you win another trophy for your shelf.

Then I found another and wished on that too
so your stomach injury heals for you,
so it doesn't cause you any more pain
and you'll win with ease,
my warrior from Spain.

Injured Knees

Rafa, you battled on like the true hero you are,
you may have lost the battle
but you've still come far;
it was awful to see you playing in pain:
I'm praying you'll soon be fit again.

Your health and fitness are top priority:
I care about you so much you see;
now take care, relax and rest,
so when you next play
you'll be at your best.

These 'Get Well' wishes to you – from me
are sent to you from over the sea;
if only I could send myself in this letter,
I'd climb right out and kiss you better!

Every Cloud Has a Silver Lining
(Roland Garros 2009)

Thinking about how the path of your career goes,
the ups and downs, the highs and lows:
your best is what you always give,
you always stay so positive.

You don't lose much, you're skilled and fit
but if you do, you learn from it:
you work on your game, on mistakes you ponder,
then next time round, you come back stronger.

I have no doubt that this is true:
come back stronger is what you'll do;
perhaps you wanted to win so much,
you got nervous and lost your touch.

I share your sadness at your loss today
but I have faith, next time you play,
everything will all work out,
you'll win again, I have no doubt.

In each experience is hidden a treasure,
what you gain from this will be beyond measure:
from this experience you will grow
into a better version of yourself, you know.

Now you're home with family and friends,
that's the best medicine to help make amends:
and all your fans are on your side,
you can still hold your head up with pride.

You took it so well; you were brave in defeat,
a more beautiful person would be hard to meet;
you're our hero whether you win or not –
for the person you are and the character you've got.

A Blessing in Disguise

You feel everything's against you,
you can't do what you want to do:
you feel your body's let you down,
cross and sad, you want to frown.

Things are spiraling out of control,
your knees are stopping you reaching your goal;
you worked so hard to reach the top,
now you're frustrated at having to stop:
but now you've put it to the test,
you know your body needs more rest.

Try to chill out, relax, that's the key,
a blessing in disguise is what this could be;
rest and heal, don't feel down in the dumps,
then the injury won't recur every few months.

You've already had it in February 09,
now it's back, lasting longer this time,
so try not to rush it, you've done the right thing:
in the long term, more success, this will bring.

To play at Wimbledon, you really did yearn,
but by missing it you'll be stronger when you return:
your body will thank you for letting it heal
and reward you with fitness, now that's a good deal!

I hate to think of you feeling so sad,
I hope my words make you feel less bad:
I'm sure that the rain cloud over your head
will have a silver lining instead.

Listening to your body was the right thing to do:
letting it rest will be good for you;
when you come back, I'll still be here,
you're the only one I'll ever cheer.

Tennis is not the same without you,
so hope and wait is what I'll do;
you're the only one that I'll support,
I hope you'll soon be back on court!

Plea to Rafa's Knees (2009)

Hear my pleas:
get well knees,
get better please,
carry him overseas,
no pain please,
fulfil his needs:
let him play with ease
and run at great speeds
and win Wimbledon, please!
(They didn't listen,
he couldn't play,
we were all so sad
it turned out that way).

Hero

You battled like the true hero you are,
you may have lost, but you've come far.

Each time you play, you give all you've got,
you're only human, not a robot!

No one can win all the time,
losing sometimes is not a crime;

I love you whether you win or not,
in me, a true fan, you have got.

My Heart is With You

I hate to think of you feeling so sad,
I wish I could help, so you don't feel so bad:
all I can do from England is pray
and write these words to ease your way.

It's a tough time that you're going through,
so hope and pray is what I'll do;
if I've helped ease your troubled soul
then I have reached my aim and goal.

You help me when I'm feeling blue,
I hope I've done the same for you,
even though I'm miles away,
I'm with you in spirit, every day.

If I can help you to feel a little better,
then I'll be so glad I sent this letter;
if you feel happiness has gone astray,
my heart is with you, and there it will stay.

Missing Rotterdam and Dubai

You did the right thing,
better safe than sorry –
no more forehands,
no more volleys;
protecting your knees
was the right thing to do:
we don't want more
injuries for you.
Winning can wait,
you'll do it real soon,
and face up at the net,
like duel at high noon.

Missing You

Missing you like mad,
been feeling so sad,
when you're better
I'll be so glad;
my love for you
is no passing fad:
my support always,
is what you'll have.

Injury Time Out

I've missed you so much
but you've worked out a plan,
that'll make you more likely
to win more of the slams:
so when you come back
you'll be fresh every day,
with priorities changed
it'll all go your way.

Good Vibes

Longing for news Rafa.
Got the blues Rafa.

Checking your website
a hundred times a day:
we've got withdrawal symptoms,
it's so long since you've played.

Want you to be well Rafa.
Miss you, can't you tell Rafa.

Watching DVD's of you
to get us through the day,
waiting till the next time
you're fit enough to play.

For you we'll always be there Rafa
and for ever we will care Rafa.

Wherever you may be
and whatever you may do,
you'll not only be there,
you're in all of our hearts too.

Love you forever Rafa.
Whatever the weather Rafa.

If rain clouds fill your mind
and you're feeling sad and blue,
always remember Rafa,
your fans are here for you.

We wish you health and joy Rafa.
You're the real McCoy Rafa.

We want to make you happy,
if sad and low you feel,
never forget that Rafa,
if life gives you a raw deal.

We believe in you Rafa.
We'll never leave Rafa.

For every one that doubts you,
there're hundreds more that don't:
we outnumber all those doubters
so bring you down, they won't!

We'll help you all we can Rafa.
We'll always be your fans Rafa.

We'll be your secret weapon
and knowing that we're there,
you'll gather all the good vibes sent
and win again with flair.

We Feel for You

We really feel what you're going through,
we hope that soon you won't feel so blue:
you've had to deal with a titanic blow;
but you'll always have our support you know.

You're loved and missed more than words can say,
we'll be cheering you on, next time you play;
we'll be so happy when you play again,
fresh and fit with no more pain.

Good News, Rafa

We're so happy that you've had
good news about your knees,
you can start practicing on Monday;
we're all so very pleased.

Arnold said, "I'll be back,"
in 'The Terminator,'
your rivals know that too:
they'd rather you're spectator!

They know when you're fit
their chances are slimmer:
more often than not
it's you that's the winner.

Injury time out is a good motivator,
soon you'll be back as the dominator!
This time out will have helped you I'm sure,
you'll soon bring more trophies
home through your door!

Your rivals will need a respirator,
Vamos Rafa; our gladiator!

Vamos Carefully

Now you're back and training again,
I hope you feel good and are feeling no pain;
it must be hard to take things slow
when you're used to giving your all, I know.

You don't want to give it your all just yet
and jeopardize your healing, as that you'd regret;
to see you at your best, we're as eager as you
so 'Vamos Rafa,' but be careful too!

We'll wait for you for as long as it takes
so don't rush it Rafa, think of the stakes!

More Bad Luck

2014 didn't go as you'd hoped,
your appendix flared up;
I don't know how you coped
on antibiotics and playing in pain:
you've showed you've got guts again and again.

Unfortunately the World Tour Finals were out;
as well as your appendix,
but you didn't hang about;
as soon as you were able
you were back on your feet:
practicing on the court,
you wanna be the man to beat.

After time out your confidence left,
nerves on big points
meant you couldn't play your best:
you were losing to rivals you normally beat,
you had to suffer more defeats;
but through it all you stayed motivated,
your determination was 'A' rated,
you 'vamosed' and ran all round the joint –
it's not over till the very last point.

Chapter Four – The Comeback

After injury Rafa comes back, trying to get back into the swing of things and to get more matches under his belt to get back to playing his best level of tennis. After some layoffs he's come back and won everything but others have been more difficult and he suffered a loss of confidence and losses to players that he normally beats: but Rafa never gives up and is highly motivated to get back to his top level of tennis and win more tournaments.

The Comeback

I'm so happy that you're ready to compete,
but opponents are circling like sharks chasing meat:
they think their best chance to beat you is now –
but you have other ideas; that's your vow.

They might not be betting on you, but don't worry,
you'll soon make them eat their words in a hurry:
a couple more contests down the line,
you'll be winning again, time after time.

You're fresh and fit and mentally strong,
they'll know you're the best before very long;
the opponents will be scared it's you they'll meet:
as they'll be the ones facing defeat.

Forget the last two months when you were down,
soon you'll be claiming another crown:
you'll show your critics, it's not your demise,
you'll be winning again and feeling so high.

If they expect you to lose, there'll be less pressure,
and after time off, you'll come back fresher,
and your secret weapon is us, all in tune,
sending good vibes to help you get through.

We're Here for You, Rafa

Coming back after injury, you might feel stressed
with speculation rife from websites and press:
they say you'll be vulnerable and won't be the same,
but there's more than one way to win at this game;
even if it's true it won't be for ever –
your tennis is smarter, your tactics are clever.

We won't pressure you to win right away you know,
we understand it'll take time for momentum to flow:
all that matters to us, is you get back good feelings,
so you can build on that and continue your healing.

You'll never disappoint us: you always do your best,
we won't pressure you; we're not like the rest,
so whenever you compete, we'll be on your side:
we'll always be here, cheering with pride.

We love you so much, we feel protective,
silencing your critics is our main objective;
obviously we love you and want you to win
but if you don't, it's not a sin!

The Comeback (Montreal)

Missed you madly,
welcome you gladly,
happy you're back,
you, we lacked;
missed your style
by a country mile,
back on court,
excitement you've brought.
Slowly, surely,
knees were poorly;
we all yearn,
good feelings to return:
when they do,
they'll all fear you.
For you we felt,
match under belt,
needn't have worried,
demolition was hurried:
performance polished,
opponent abolished!

The Bull is Back

Woke from slumber,
wolf like hunger,
quenched my thirst,
onto court you burst;
incredible belief,
sigh of relief,
knees held out,
no more doubts.
Now knees are mended
play's not suspended,
confidence growing,
good feelings are showing;
tennis is exciting
now you're back fighting.
Warrior mentality,
amazing tenacity;
Spanish bull,
exceptional.

Improving After Injury

In your blog you said
we're sharp with our questions,
well you're sharp with your tennis too:
watching your second round match,
we were amazed at what you could do.

Rafa, you're looking so good out there,
your game's so precise
with strokes full of flair:
we can see the determination
and the focus that's in you;
you're improving so much,
we hope it continues.

With each match you win,
so loud we do cheer,
you'll hear us in America
from way over here!
Good luck in round three
when you're on court today;
I hope you win the tournament,
it'd really make my day!

Relentless Rafa – Keeps on Coming at Ya!

It's a battle of skill and a battle of wills:
Rafa runs 'em ragged so it's all up hill;
mucho winners from the racket of remarkable Rafa:
his rivals all realize that he keeps on coming at ya –
Relentless Rafa; just keeps on coming at ya!

If Rafa's ever behind in the score,
it just means he'll raise his game a little bit more;
he might be down but there's hunger in his eyes:
he's very good at bouncing back,
he'll take you by surprise –
Relentless Rafa; just keeps on coming at ya!

If he doesn't make it and he ends up as the loser,
he works and learns and next time round
he battles like a bruiser!
Relentless Rafa; just keeps on coming at ya!

The few times he gets beaten,
it doesn't get him down,
his self-belief and positivity
means he'll win next time around –
Relentless Rafa; just keeps on coming at ya!

After all his injuries in 2009
he worked his famous arse off
and now he's winning all the time!
Relentless Rafa; just keeps on coming at ya!

Rafa – Put on Your Poker Face

Rafa put on your poker face
and serve them up a topspin ace;

if you're anxious, don't let it show,
pretend you're confident, so they don't know:

'fake it till you feel,' it is what they say;
soon you'll feel confident every day;

you're starting to rebuild your armour
to get that feeling that 'no one can harm ya,'

you've done it before and you'll do it again,
I know that you'll solve it –
you're my hero from Spain!

Coming Back Again

Losses to players you normally beat
and a loss of confidence too,
made it a very difficult task
to get back on track for you;

your body language stayed the same,
you knew it could change in a minute,
your best tennis will surface again,
and soon you'll be the one that'll win it!

You gained even more admiration
from every one of your fans,
what you're going through, we share with you,
sending support, is the job in our hands.

If we can help in some small way,
it's what we wanna do,
you're the one we love the most –
our love for you is true.

Chapter Five – Rafa and His Rivals

Matches between rivals are always special and exciting. Rafa has had some fantastic duels and these matches bring out strong feelings in his fans.

Rafa's head to head with some of his rivals at the time of writing:

Nadal 23	Federer	11
Nadal 23	Djokovic	25
Nadal 14	Warwinka	3
Nadal 16	Murray	6
Nadal 24	Ferrer	6
Nadal 19	Berdych	4
Nadal 6	Soderling	2
Nadal 4	Rosol	1
Nadal 6	Fogninni	3
Nadal 7	Roddick	3
Nadal 16	Verdasco	3
Nadal 8	Nishikori	1
Nadal 9	Lopez	4
Nadal 5	Karlovic	0

Rafa and his Rivals

Djokovic, Federer and Murray's in the mix,
Beating any of these rivals gives Rafael his kicks;
the head to head ratio is mostly in Rafa's favour,
even through bad times, he has great wins to savour;
he keeps his hopes alive and never gives up:
he always has belief that he'll win another cup.

After losing 2 finals, to win Wimbledon he did strive,
in 2008 he did it, beating Federer in five;
he beat Fed again in Australia 2009,
another classic win brought Fed to tears that time;
Olympic gold semi, beating Novak in 2008 –
Rafa's had significant wins and losing was their fate!

Magnifico Matador

Why's Federer on the floor?
It's our hunky matador,
he's passed him at the net
(he'd better watch his castanets!)
as our Spaniard is so hot,
he's got Federer's legs in knots!

The bull's back to his best,
Federer needs a little rest,
Rafa's charging like a stag,
Federer's waving the white flag:
all he can do is surrender
and return to his hacienda!

Resting Rafa

'Wish you were here' is what postcards say,
well I wish I was here with you today,

Rafa it looks like you're having such fun:
in the sea, on the boat in the Mallorcan sun.

A well-deserved rest is just what you need,
fun with your friends will help you indeed,

so you'll be fresh as a fish when you're playing again,
ready to take over from Novak's rein:

you'll work out solutions
and come to conclusions,
on how to metaphorically clobber him –
so your game will again bother him,
and you'll be the one stopping him!

Enjoy your rest Rafa, you're the best Rafa,
you'll be well rested and you'll get your wish
to win The French Open: our mouths will be open,
watching your skill, as you go in for the kill,
the champion is you, you're the winner it's true!

Hope for Rafa

Rafa, don't say that you can't beat Novak;
tomorrow is another day:
no one works harder and smarter than you,
I'm sure you'll win next time you play.

Don't let him get right into your head,
don't let him mess with your mind,
you're fans will always be here for you,
we're sure you can kick his behind!

I know your resolution is to find a solution
and when you do, we'll be thrilled for you;
so get back to it –
we know you can do it!

You'll Win Again

Almost 25 and already 9 slams,
19 Masters 1000's you hold in your hands;
so much you've achieved and you're not done yet,
Roland Garros is the next chance you'll get –

then there's Queens and Wimbledon too,
I'm confident you'll work out what to do
to beat Novak again, and put him back in his place,
you're smart, you work hard and your talent is ace!

So 'Vamos' Rafa, I'm fighting with you,
with every breath that I have too,
I'm hoping and praying with all my heart,
your winning run is about to start;

and one thing you can definitely count on
is whatever happens, I'll never be gone,
I'll always be here with support just for you,
each round that you play, I hope you get through.

Someday soon you'll work it out,
you'll take Novak down without a doubt;
that day'll be sooner than he thinks,
and down the rankings he will sink;
you'll be rising higher every day –
your new found game'll blow him away.

Rafa Rocks

The prerequisite
to be exquisite
is practice innit!

You practice a lot,
that's why you're so hot –
I got the hots
for your sexy bot
and those outrageous shots!

Truly magnificent talent
and a gentleman so gallant;
a stunning point –
you rock the joint!

Your tennis is breathtaking,
Djokovic you'll be replacing,
as the new No.1;
Rafa your time will soon come.

Rafa You'll Always be Our No.1

Rafa our hearts go out to you today,
we're always proud of you, come what may;
we know you're disappointed, we are too,
but we're never disappointed in you;
you fight so hard and try your best
on every point, you never rest,
so don't you worry, we'll always be here,
it's you that we all want to cheer.

I know that soon the day will come
when you beat Novak and end his run
of wins against you, if time you bide,
the law of averages is on your side,
and when that day comes, we'll all celebrate,
in our book it'll be a special date,
one we'll remember, when the tide turned,
a wonderful date for which we all yearned;
Rafa I know your day will come
when you win again and regain No.1.

Don't be too sad, you'll work it out,
of that I'm sure, I have no doubt;
you've had tough times and you've come through,
there'll be more good times ahead of you,
and we'll be here to share your joy,
our Spanish hero, you're the real McCoy;
you set a good example every minute,
your reward will come, next time you'll win it!

A Match at High Noon

Tomorrow Rafa you'll have no pressure,
tomorrow, playing will be a pleasure,
tomorrow you'll manage to win,
come what may,
tomorrow's a new season,
a fresh start, a new day;
tomorrow is when you'll break that curse:
it'll be Novak who comes off worst!

Your skill and determination
will help you through it,
and when you win I'll say, 'I knew it!'
I knew you could do it,
and all your other fans knew too,
wherever you're playing
we'll always cheer you;
tomorrow we'll have lots to cheer about
as Rafa, your shots have a whole lotta clout!

Novak just won't be able to hack it
as your passing shot flies past his racket;
so remember be calm, focused and sure,
you can run him ragged till he's on the floor!
Stick to your game plan,
believe in yourself:
tomorrow,
a new trophy will be on your shelf.

Aussie Open Final – Rafa Did Us Proud

Don't be too disappointed,
please don't be sad,
there're a whole lot of positives to be had:
I hope that you gain mucho confidence today;
the day you beat Novak is not far away:
the fighting qualities you showed were brilliant
and next time you'll be even more resilient;
you're building towards a fantastic moment
when you beat your most difficult opponent.
Rafa you're getting better and closer
to beating the Novak and giving him a dosa
his own medicine, cos you *will* beat him,
when you do it'll be your sweetest win.
You've gained points and improved;
determination you exude,
when you beat him it'll be a rude
awakening!
He thinks he's untouchable,
made of steel or tin,
but you're closing in
on a satisfying win.
Rafa don't be more than a little bit sad,
cos you're getting closer to beating him
and for that we're all glad.
Novak knows you're close on his heels,
now more confident, is how you feel;
you're on the up and Novak will frown,
cos soon he'll be on the way down!
Now you're more competitive,
soon your wins will be repetitive;
you're motivated, dedicated;

watching, we're intoxicated;
exciting, fighting, amazing striking;
topspin down the line,
incredible shot making, just sublime:
Rafael – you will prevail.

Miami Final 2011

Novak is still in his purple patch,
but even so it was a very close match,
it really could've gone either way,
don't be too sad about your loss today;

you still got further than you did last year,
and soon we'll be crying happier tears,
cos on the clay you'll beat 'em all,
it's your rivals turn to take a fall!

Novak's on Borrowed Time (Rome 2011)

Rafa I'm glad that sad's *not* how you're feeling,
you're an example of an admirable human being,
and one thing you can definitely count on
is whatever happens, we'll never be gone –

we'll always be here with support just for you,
today our love and respect just grew:
the way you fought and never gave up,
you'll get your reward and bite another cup.

When you do it'll mean much more
because you'll have won a difficult war;
we're so proud of you for the person you are:
win or lose, you're our shining star.

We love you Rafa, never forget it,
supporting you, we'll never quit!
I know that you'll work out how to beat Novak,
and very soon you'll be back on track.

Indian Wells Final (2011)

This year you made the final,
after last year only semi,
you've improved and gained points;
don't be sad – well not very!

You didn't play well in the final set,
but next time you will, on that I'll bet;
Novak won Indian Wells in 2008
but it was one of your best years;
you still did great,
him winning today doesn't mean diddly-squat,
cos you can beat anyone when your tennis is hot;
you can be confident that you can go up a gear
and beat him next time you meet this year.

Novak's in a purple patch,
there's not much you could do,
but soon you'll be in a purple patch too;
I don't need to say, 'Don't lose heart,'
you've improved on last year's result
and it's only the start;
I have faith that you'll do fine,
and you'll be the one that wins next time.

Rafa Will Rule in Rome

The run Novak's on just can't continue,
and you're the one to stop it,
it's in every sinew
of muscle you have,
to fight till the last
breath, that is his –
off the court he'll be blast.

Today is your day,
the last day of the week,
to show that pretender,
it was just a lucky streak,
but his luck will run out,
the King's back in town
to claim back his crown
and knock Novak right down,
a peg or two, back to his place;
then balance will be restored –
I rest my case.

So 'Vamos' Rafa, we're fighting with you
with every breath that we have too,
praying and cheering with all our hearts
your winning run is about to start!

Monte Carlo or Bust

Rafa in peach and he's peachy keen,
Monte Carlo titles, 8 he did glean;
20 Masters 1000 titles,
he's won all those too:
he's ahead of the rest –
his records are too!

Beating Novak after 7 losses straight,
I knew this was the day, this was the date:
after Australia he knew he could do it,
with confidence back,
no one could say that he blew it;
Australia was a 'good loss;'
and that paved the way
for Rafa's great victory over Novak today.

Rafa Beat Novak

Rain delayed play,
but it didn't stop you today,
nothing could stop your plans
to hold that trophy in your hands.

You came on court determined
and ran around like a whirlwind,
you wouldn't let your chance slip by,
tonight Rafa, we're all so high;

happy you retained your crown,
now its Novak's turn to frown;
you've showed them all who is the best –
you're a class above him
and all the rest.

A Rafan's Dilemma

Just don't know
which way to go,
lesser of two evils –
wish it was a no show!

Fed or Novak?
Novak or Fed?
Which winner is better for Rafa?
Which one's hopes should I put to bed?

18 Grand slams for Fed on the line,
pulling away from Rafa's 14
to be The Greatest of All Time;
No.1 for Novak
means he'll turn up the heat,
more confidence in future
so he's harder for Rafa to beat!

An awful dilemma for Rafans,
I wish it was an easier choice:
if Dimitrov had beaten Novak,
I'd be cheering *him* at the top of my voice!

Rafa v Verdasco (Indian Wells 15/3/16)

After losing to Nando in Australia
a couple of months ago,
Rafa was drawn to play him again
and this time was raring to go!

Rafa changed his strings again,
it made his topspin faster;
it was at least 200 revolutions more,
of his craft, he is the master.

Rafa was on fire tonight,
determined, calm and steady;
whoever he meets at Indian Wells,
to kick their arse, he's ready!

He won set 1, 6 games to love,
he bageled Nando properly;
I'm sure he's determined in his head,
'no one's gonna stop me.'

In set 2 Nando put up a fight,
he broke Rafa then Rafa broke back:
at 6 games all, it was tie break time,
Rafa won, and he'll be back!

Chapter Six – The Rafa Effect

This chapter is about the effect Rafa has on us fans: his sexiness and the way he makes our daydreams X-rated!

The Rafa Effect

First a Pop video so raunchy,
it made us feel naughty,
our desire for him we just can't hide;

then pictures in underwear,
a treat that's so rare:
now scantily clad Rafa, we've eyed.

No more can I write
for fear that I might
be deleted for being too sexy –
cos that's the way Rafa affects me!

Watching Rafa in 'Gypsy'

The space between
seems way too far –
it needs correcting;
rejecting's not an option:
it's in your fate,
create some magic;
exotic whisper,
kiss her tenderly,
sending me;
ahhh,
far away….
wish it was me:
he aims to please.

Raunchy Rafa

Seeing you in a Pop video is really fantastic:
we're all having daydreams – they're very romantic;
we all want to take the place of Shakira
and get closer to you – we want to get nearer!

Seeing you looking romantic and raunchy
is making my thoughts get so very naughty:
in my dreams it's me you're romancing;
gazing up at your eyes, my heart won't stop dancing.

We slowly rub noses then our lips press together:
your hungry kisses are soft as a feather,
you bite my lip so sexy and gentle,
I want you so much it's driving me mental!

Ooohh Rafa, just look at what you're doing:
you're more addictive than mothers ruin!
How I wish it was me that you're wooing!

I hope to see more of you looking like this –
then all my daydreams would have me in bliss!

The Armani Effect

Rafa, when you made TV ads for Armani jeans
and posed for photos in undies to go in magazines,
all your female fans were feeling so glad
that you posed for those pictures so scantily clad!

To tell of my daydreams I dare not speak
as I gaze at your gorgeous hunky physique:
my heart beats faster, I'm sizzling hot;
that's how you affect me with the body you've got!

In your Armani clothes you look classy and hot,
we love everything about you, you've got the lot!
Your jeans look great on that famous arse,
and whatever you wear, you ooze style and class;
modeling those undies you gave us a thrill;
Rafa we love you, you just look so brill –
and all the ladies wanna get their fill!

It's not just me, other ladies feel the same:
you really know how to ignite the flame
of passion and longing and yearning and love,
we feel it for you; no one else is above:
you're our No.1 in all that you do,
the most beautiful person – Rafa that's you!

The Tommy Hilfiger Effect

Rafa in Tommy Hilfiger
well this campaign sure looks bigger;

is it the cut of the pants
that makes ya give a 2nd glance?

Is he enjoying his work so much
his photos just don't need re-touch!

The fragrance is Bold and so is he,
I wish he'd come and be bold with me!

His skin covers hills and peaks
smooth and sleek:

over muscles shapely,
I don't feel saintly:

let my lips
kiss valleys and dips;

smooth as stones,
bronzed and toned;

golden as sand, velvet soft;
Vincent Van Gogh,

would paint you –
that's so true.

Good Luck now it's Back to Business

Since you last played a long time has passed by:
at the Australian Open you made me so high,
answering my questions on 'The Herald' online,
I was so happy that you answered mine:
especially the answer when I asked how you felt
knowing ladies wanna marry you;
you just make us melt!
You said, "To go that much further
we'd have to know each other more,"
well I'm ready and willing if you knock on my door!

Being an actor is what you did next:
some of your fans were rather perplexed;
but most of us love it; you gave us a treat,
you really know how to turn up the heat!

The camera loves you and we all do too:
to be your leading lady, we're forming a queue!
I hope it's something that you'll repeat:
other leading men just can't compete,
as you're tough yet cute, sexy yet shy
and your beautiful smile lights up the night sky;
there's just no hope for all the rest,
cos Rafa – it's *so* clear you're the best!

Now you're back on court again,
back to business to continue your reign;
the other players won't know what's hit 'em:
History books will be re-written;
in years to come, it'll say you were the best –
you're a cut above the rest!

Sexy, Spanish and Spoken For

Xisca is so lucky,
as Rafa is her man,
millions wanna kiss him
but she's the only one that can!

Rafa is so hunky
and bronzed from the Mallorcan sun,
but he's sexy, Spanish and spoken for –
I wish I was the lucky one!

For a cute laugh and a flashing smile,
amongst all the others I'd queue for miles;
to get close to him my heart would pound,
but he has a tight circle of family around;

and one day too he'll have a wife
and kids, but no dogs as they frighten the life
out of him, as much as the dark does and
I wish I was there to hold his hand!

Rafael, For You We Fell

He knows that we love him,
no one is above him,
he can tell by the things that we write;

we've been fans for years,
through laughter and tears,
and to watch him is such a delight.

His play is exciting
and just as enticing
are the jobs that he does on the side:

a Pop video so raunchy,
it made us feel naughty,
our desire for him we just cannot hide!

Now a model for underwear:
almost everything bare,
in our dreams for that we had waited:

now he's done it; it's real
and the way that we feel
is making our daydreams X-rated!

Magnifico yet Modest Mallorcan

With an aura so radiant and humble,
drenched in the smell of success:
your smile and charisma so charming;
I'm in love – I have to confess!

A wonderful groundhog day,
each time better than the last:
you're leaving a trail of amazing history
behind you; in your past.

Never before has there been
one as magnetic as you,
we know a good soul when we see one –
you're an 'Earth Angel' all the way through!

Mysterious Mallorcan

Mysterious Mallorcan, I love your style,
the way you tease makes me smile:
you keep us all guessing about what's in store,
you leave us all wanting that little bit more!

You say it's a long story, you failing P.E.,
so I'm left in suspense: will you ever tell me?
(How 'bout letting me know over a nice cuppa tea!)
For the mixed doubles question,
you've gone telepathic, it's clear;
you said you knew what we wanted to hear.
Sleeveless tops, maybe yes, maybe no,
you're driving us crazy
with your teasing you know!

Rafa, let me tell you, you're so lovely with it,
as we hang onto your every word
of charismatic wit;
your humour and charisma
is really so attractive,
I can't help flirting with you,
I wish you'd be reactive!

You really are so sexy,
I'm so in love with you,
I'm falling deeper every minute,
what's a girl to do?
I'd better change the subject,
I'm so getting carried away;
I hope you win the tournament,
It'd really make my day!

Carried Away (again!)

Mysterious Spaniard,
smouldering and tough,
of your love, I can't get enough.
(In my dreams!)

Sultry, sexy, cute and shy,
you're all these things,
for your kiss I would die.
(What a way to go!)

Enchanting, intoxicating,
intriguing, charismatic,
if only my love wasn't one way traffic.
(I should be so lucky!)

I think your tummy's really yummy,
everytime I see it I go all funny!
(Don't call the Doctor, it's only love!)

You're in such good shape, Rafa,
fancy a date Rafa?
(I don't mean the edible kind!)

If you ordered pizza
from the menu at eight,
would you bite me too
if I arrived with your plate?
(I wish!)
(Man cannot live on bread alone!)

Fruits of My Labour

Apple of my eye,
peachy bum,
I feel fruity,
love your tum!
Raspberry tart,
strawberry fool,
banana split,
really cool.
Plum in my mouth,
skinless grapes,
pear and apricot,
mouth water makes.
Load of nonsense
with nectarine,
tastes much better
with ice-cream!
Knickerbocker Glory
in a frosted glass,
Rafa I love
your famous arse!

No Shirt Practice

No shirt practice, what a treat:
your fans think your body can't be beat;
we can't stop looking, don't be amazed
if some of your fans end up looking dazed!

When you change your shirt, you look so fine,
do it slow Rafa, take your time!
That could apply to other things too –
if we were alone, just me and you!

How I Imagine I'd Feel if I Met Rafa

Your words caress my ears,
the emotion moves me to tears,
your accent drives me crazy,
your voice makes me go hazy:
to be coherent I endeavour
but I can't even string
a sentence together!
Your face is mesmerizing,
my brain's gone into hiding,
your body's so attractive
(I dream you'll be reactive!)
I mustn't think thoughts of that kind:
just in case you read my mind,
your soulful eyes might read my face
and think that I'm a right disgrace!
My heart's on my sleeve,
I know you can see,
I can't help dreaming
of you loving me.
I bet this happens to you a lot,
so many women,
love what you've got:
you're somebody special
and they can all see –
millions of women
feel just like me!

Perfect Portrayal

Sexy, beaming,
full of feeling;
soulful, mysterious,
focused and serious;
laid back and funny,
personality sunny;
charismatic charm,
wise and calm;
sporty, active,
very attractive;
oh so hunky,
dances funky;
captivating, adorable,
mesmerizing, applaudable;
tantalizing, teasing,
gorgeous, pleasing;
sultry, astute,
stylish and cute;
beautiful, endearing,
fascinating, appealing:
desirable Rafael,
perfect portrayal;
superlatives apt,
that's a fact.

Why Do We Love You, Rafa?

Your skin, your eyes,
your bum, your thighs,
your cheeks, your lips,
your back, your hips;
your chest, your arms,
your smile, your charms,
your abs, your calves,
your voice, your laugh;
your face, your hair,
your style, your flair,
your fingers, your hands,
your kindness to fans;
your compassion, your grace
to the whole Human Race.
That's why!

Your Face

Strong jawline revealed
when head's thrown back,
beautiful bone structure,
other players lack;
neck revealed,
need to nuzzle,
(in my dreams!)
it's no puzzle:
it's as plain
as your beautiful nose,
I love you from
your head to your toes.
Prominent cheekbones,
perfectly formed,
beautiful is how
you were born.
Eyes that shine,
sparkle and glow,
no wonder ladies'
love for you grows.
Cute mannerisms,
expressive eyebrow,
looking at you –
I just think 'Wow.'
A radiant smile
goes on to infinity,
lights up everywhere
in the vicinity;
like a beacon of light
it stretches for miles,
that's what it's like

to witness your smiles.
Overall your face
is the best I've seen:
looking at you
is like a dream.

In Your Eyes

My dreams begin
within your eyes,
your eyes shine,
mine love them;
brown and deep
keep your soul;
stole my heart,
impart your soul:
whole of you
through them shines:
kind by design;
time you give,
with humanity you excel,
Rafael.

Your Famous Arse

I apologize in advance if it's a bit too naughty,
but the rhyming works best and I am around 40!
You might not wanna read you're our fantasy man,
so if you wanna turn over now – you can!

A friend challenged me to write about your bum,
I had to say yes, so here's the outcome!
Your famous arse could win rear of the year,
you could win it for sure, that's very clear.

Your bum is sexy, firm and muscular,
it makes the ladies feel such lust for ya!
No one fills their shorts like you,
you give me hot flushes, what can I do?

In those shorts you look so hot,
Oh My God, what a sexy bot!
No one looks better than you in jeans,
you're so strong and hunky
you must eat all your greens!

In those tight jeans no one looks better,
just thinking about it makes me hotter & wetter!
It's not even Summer and I'm all hot and sticky:
now I'm dreaming we're having a quickie!
(but I'm not a one night stand kinda girl,
in my dreams Rafa, you love me as well –
and as all my other poems show,
it's not just your body we love, you know,
but your arse is an asset I had to include –
I hope you don't think I'm being too rude!)

Your Voice

Your 'Spanglish' is delightful,
what else can I say:
if it was whispered in just my ear,
it'd really make my day!

I love your pronunciation;
it really is endearing,
I could listen to you all day long:
I so love what I'm hearing!

The way you say *positive hacktitude*
is important for your tennis *careera*
and you've won on every *surfrace*,
(you really are superior)

I think the English dictionary
should be re-written just like this:
if everybody spoke like you
my ears would be in bliss!

The way you say *no* at the end of a line,
in England some people say *yeah,*
nobody else sounds as good as you do,
nobody else can compare.

Then there's the noise you make
when you hit the ball,
now that's the sexiest sound of all!

To other players noises
I'm indifferent or annoyed

but listening to yours
I'm feeling overjoyed!

You can tell from this poem,
I'm head over heels,
but I'm just one of millions
to whom you appeal!

Your Physique

Mid-shot your shirt flies up, as into the air you leap,
revealing your tummy, so we all get a peep;
I've seen it happen before with other players too –
but they don't have the body you do.
Your mid-section's bronzed & your six pack is hard,
some players don't have abs, all they have is lard!
Your physique is statuesque, muscular yet lean:
it's the sexiest body I've ever seen;
and I think I speak for other fans too,
as millions of us have a crush on you!

Your muscular arms are the best they could be,
how I wish you'd wrap them right around me!
Your thighs and calves are strong and muscular,
oh Rafa, I think I'm falling in love with ya!
Last but not least is your famous arse,
what can I say – it's just 1st class;
but it's not just your body I love, it's your mind:
you're funny and thoughtful and loving and kind;
such a perfect combination is hard to find!

Your Hair

You remove your headband
when the match is done,
cameras clicking all around
as to the net you run;
I love the way your hair
falls just over your eye:
your eye sparkles behind it,
so sexy, I sigh.

You shake your head,
so natural; so unaware,
how like a model you look,
I can't help but stare:
wild and sexy,
dripping with sweat,
have I mentioned
how much I love it yet?

When it's wet it looks longer
and it looks really good,
I want to run my fingers through,
if only I could;
then when it's dry,
it springs back up shorter,
you look so cute,
mothers lock up your daughters!

It's not to protect them
from a broken heart:
it's cos they're after you too,
and they want a head start!

My Muse

Looking at you, I'm so inspired,
my creative juices are all on fire:
ideas for poems, happy and tragic,
flow from my pen, as if by magic,
feelings are magnified times 102,
if I get published, it's thanks to you.

My best poems are written
with you in mind,
a better muse, I'll never find:
the best human qualities,
you have them all,
you set an angelic example
in this 'Earth School.'
You inspire others
to help like you do,
so we're all better people
as we share a love for you.

Your outer beauty draws people near,
then seeing your beautiful soul
becomes clear,
all these things are so beguiling,
an 'Earth Angel' that's so inspiring.

You inspire sculptors, poets
and artists too,
you inspire human values,
we look up to you;
you inspire people to work hard
and reach their goal,

to move forward past setbacks
and resume their role.

You inspire people in so many ways,
you're a beautiful person
who brightens our days:
you don't have to try,
you're so natural and true –
you inspire so many
by just being you.

Cheerleader Chant

R is for Rafa the one we adore,
A is for our Admiration, it grows more and more,
F is for Fighting spirit,
A is for Ace,
E is for Energy as he runs round the place.
L is for the Love and the way we all care,
N is for Nike and the clothes that he wears,
A is for Affection that we all feel for you,
D is for Dreams, we hope they come true.
A is for Accent, we love how you speak,
L is for Ladies, you make us go weak;
Rafael Nadal, you're loved by so many,
to meet you would make all our legs turn to jelly;
we love you so much, our emotions are strong,
this love will last, our whole lifetime long.

My Dream Man

Your bronzed toned skin next to mine,
our hands entwined, your kiss divine;
in my dreams you're mine.

I look up at your beautiful eyes:
hear my sighs,
my eyes are wide open, staring it's true –
I don't want to miss the beauty of you.

Your sculptured cheeks
make my heart miss a beat:
those cheekbones are so kissable,
your beauty is unmissable;
I could listen to you talking all day long,
to me it's like a sexy song:
your voice is so exotic,
it makes me feel erotic;
your biceps are so muscular
they really make me lust for ya!
Wild and sexy, that's your hair,
your beauty is beyond compare:
not just outside but inside too,
I really love the man that's you.

Chapter Seven – Essence of Rafael

This chapter is about Rafa as a person, about how kind and compassionate he is and the way he wants to improve the world by helping others with his Foundation; this man has a heart of gold.

Champions Drink Responsibly

Your new campaign is really a good cause,
to make everyone stop and pause,
to keep their drinking responsible,
knowing when to say no:
now that's a good call;
people listen to you,
you're loved and respected,
they'll think before they drink,
about who is affected,
especially if they're driving friends
home in the car,
they'll just order a fruit juice
when they're up at the bar;
they'll remember
champions drink responsibly,
the proof is Rafa,
it's clear to see!

Rafa's Legacy

You'll be remembered
as a man who is fair,
a man with compassion,
a man who cares:
your legacy will be one
that people admire,
that inspires them to do good,
to have that burning desire;
to do the right thing in all that they do,
because they've been inspired by you;
and for the world it's advantageous,
because doing the right thing
becomes contagious,
and it'll make life better for one and all,
thanks to you
and your talent with a tennis ball!
You're in a position to spread the word,
I hope that lots of people heard!
Drinking responsibly is just the start –
you do so much more
with your generous heart.

Rafa – My Ray of Sunshine

You're a ray of sunshine
in my life,
you take away worries
and illness strife;
I have renewed enthusiasm
because of you:
new goals and purpose
have seen me through.
When days are darkened
with worry and fear,
you take it away
and wipe the slate clear –
and to your foundation
I've given some money:
from my book of poems
(some are quite funny!)
I did it all
while thinking of you,
you never give up
so I wouldn't too;
this is to thank you,
you've done more than you know,
I've given a donation
so your profits will grow;
to help others in need,
like you've helped me:
now I've found joy –
and you were the key.

Inspired By Rafa

Rafa can you tell me
if you have a favorite poet?
I've written lots about you –
I wonder if you know it?

I've put some on your Facebook page
and others on your website,
I just feel I want to tell you true,
I'm so inspired by all you do.

You never give up
and you keep your goal in sight,
whenever you're knocked down,
you get back up and fight;

you inspire me so much to do that too,
now I've written three books
and it's all thanks to you.

When my first few books sold,
I donated to your foundation,
it made me so happy
to help others around the nation.

I haven't sold that many:
I've still not made a profit,
but in your footsteps I will follow
and trying – I won't stop it!

Rafa, Our National Treasure

Smile, eyes, lips,
sweet as sherbet dips.

Muscles, jaw, cheeks,
rugged as mountain peeks.

Thoughtful sensitive emotions,
feelings as deep as the oceans.

Personality friendly and fun,
warmer than the mid-day sun.

Cute accent you express,
gentle as a soft caress.

Vamos, natural and raw
as a wave crashing on the shore.

To watch him is such a pleasure,
he's like a National Treasure.

Universal Spaniard

Rafa, you're a diamond,
you're worth your weight in gold,
your kindness shows no boundaries,
you're loved by young and old.

Thoughtful and considerate,
an empath, through and through,
the beauty on your outside,
goes deep inside you too.

You teach by example
and show others how to be,
caring, kind and helpful
towards all humanity.

A Master of Compassion,
a higher calling than the rest,
your attitude to life
inspires us to do our best.

Bringing out the best in others
just by being you,
gives us higher standards
that we want to live up to.

Your good influence is powerful,
it goes all around the globe
and winning 'Universal Spaniard'
shows you're a natural on that road.

Universal Appeal

A will of steel, Universal appeal,
a heart of gold, a sight to behold.

He's great with children,
they copy him with glee,
there's no greater role model
they could want to be.

Teenage girls have fallen in love:
they think Rafa's been sent from above.

40 something's are smitten as well,
it's for Rafa, that they've fell.

The over 60's love him too:
they saw his humanity
and their love for him grew.

This man is beautiful inside and out,
all ages agree, of that there's no doubt.

My Sporting Hero

A will of steel,
Universal appeal,
a heart of gold,
a sight to behold;
a man I love,
sent from above:
humanity and charm,
laid back and calm:
he radiates charisma,
a warm feeling he gives ya;
unique, special, one of a kind,
this man is always on my mind,
and as well as all that –
what a sexy behind!

Rafa Removes My Woe

I dunno, I find it all so,
well you know just 'so so,'
I feel no 'way to go,'
feeling such woe,
being so low,
squashes joy so it can't grow;
but then I'm feeling happier, 'no?'
listening to Rafa removes my woe.

Angel Heart

Rafael, you share your name with an Angel,
you have the heart of one too:
helping to make a better world,
thinking of others more than you.

You must be an 'Earth Angel' the things that you do,
so many people are grateful to you:
you give your time even when you are busy,
signing autographs in every city.

Charity work comes natural, it's true
helping others satisfies you;
and as well as all that, your matches they thrill,
watching your tennis, enjoying such skill,
gives people pleasure, takes worries away,
you accomplish so much, day after day;
you give so much more than you probably know,
so this poem says thanks to our Angelic Pro!

A Hug in Words

I wanted to write a poem
about how you make me feel:

full of beautiful words and emotions
to show how much you appeal;

but the words haven't yet been invented,
you're more beautiful than I can describe:

the essence of Rafael Nadal
gives such a positive vibe!

Rafa – A Beautiful Soul

Rafa you're lovely,
your picture's above me:
I'm looking at you as I write;
your spirit shines through
when I look at you –
it shines from your soul clear and bright.

To do the right thing
makes your heart sing;
you spread joy wherever you go;
compassion and love
is what you're made of:
that's the reason why I love you so.

You're Our Everything Rafa

We love your body,
we love your mind,
we love your personality;
in fact you'll find
we love your everything,
you're everything to us,
everything about you
is a capital A plus!

We love your tennis
and the way you move;
not just on court
but your mannerisms too:
we can't take our eyes
off your expressive face,
we long for your arms
and their warm embrace;

your charisma and kindness
and beautiful smile,
have been melting our hearts
for a very long while;
you're our everything,
you're everything to us,
we can't help loving you:
in fact – it's a must.

Interaction on Facebook
and 'The Times' online:
you're a beautiful person
for giving your time;

interviews on TV
and in magazines,
autographs and photos:
so much it means;

we appreciate so much
everything you do;
you're our everything –
everything is you.

Thanks for All You Do Rafa

I went onto facebook
and was so pleased to find
a video from Rafa –
you're one of a kind;
it's so lovely that you keep in touch,
as a fan I appreciate it very much.

Muchas gracias Rafa
for all that you do,
my support will always be for you:
no other player tugs at my heartstrings like you!

Rafa – Best of Everything Rolled into One

You whip the ball to an amazing angle:
your racket flies round ya head;
it never gets in a tangle!

High bounce; topspin;
accurate execution:
the opponent just can't find the solution.

Exciting to watch, power and precision:
watching you's a no brainer decision;
I'd choose to watch you every time,
you're a treat for the eyes; your game is sublime.

That's not all you've got going for you
with your sexy mannerisms and charisma too;
your humble personality and kindness to fans,
the way you help others in far off lands:
you're a wonderful person with a heart of gold,
all the best qualities, into you, are rolled!

Rafa – My Inspirational Earth Angel

You're so respected; when you speak, heads turn,
from your words and actions
the whole world can learn:
integrity, empathy, compassion, humility,
the qualities you have, show your divinity.

People admire you and look up to you
and want to help others, the way that you do;
you inspire me in life to keep on trying,
the problems I have cause pain and crying,
but you cheer me up and make me smile again,
your angelic qualities ease my pain.

Yesterday I was crying a lot
but watching your match, I soon forgot;
I feel so blessed at what you do for me,
now my book is published, it's clear to see,
people with problems can still accomplish dreams,
if I can spread that message, and some beams;
I'll be helping others to do the same
and put sunshine where there once was rain.

If I can spread a little happiness the way that you do,
then I'll be satisfied when my life is through.

Don't Give Up – Rafa Wouldn't

Change?
Will I be able to?
Law unto myself.

Don't abuse your chances
or neglect to dot the i's,
pay attention to the finer details –
don't just roll the dice.

Make it happen, you can do it,
you're stronger than you think,
and if you fail to reach your goal,
just go and have a drink (of tea!)

Don't give up cos Rafa wouldn't;
just do like he does,
there's no way you won't feel inspired,
he gives you such a buzz!

Somewhere deep inside,
you will detect a spark:
fan the flame and watch it grow
and leave behind the dark.

There's always hope, just watch Rafa
and you'll see it's true;
I don't just mean in tennis –
I mean your whole life through.

Essence of Rafael

Spiritual Soul,
Wise One,
keeps on learning,
it's never done.

Inner Voice,
life enhancer:
listen closely,
avoid disaster.

Admitting Mistakes,
learning from them:
doing the same thing,
never again.

Spiritual Development,
soul is learning:
moving forward
in the journeying.

Emotional Intelligence,
highly advanced:
empathetic in
right circumstance.

Humanitarian Visionary,
kind and caring:
suffering in others,
he is sparing.

Foundation Created,

shows compassion:
help for others
is not rationed.

All these things
make up his essence,
bottle and drink:
Learn The Lessons.

Drink in his essence,
picture his face,
take on his values:
World's a Better Place.

Bottle and wrap,
give as presents:
Nothing Better
than His Essence.

Transformation
then takes place,
all across
the Human Race.

Chapter Eight – A Fan's Feelings

This chapter is about how I, and many others feel about Rafa, I think you'll identify with the poems in this chapter if you're a fan of Rafa's.

A Fan's Feelings

There you are, here I am,
thinking of you, but I'm just a fan;
falling for you, more each day,
praying you'll win, each time you play.

Can I be your favourite fan?
One in a million so you know who I am.
Can I be your 'virtual' best friend
and write notes to you at the days end?

Can I send you poems to brighten your day
and 'Good Luck' messages each time you play?
Will you look forward to hearing from me?
Your special supporter from over the sea!

Seeing your messages and photos
is so exciting to all of your fans,
this poem is just to say thank you –
you're a thoughtful and beautiful man.

Reading your facebook page
really brightens our day:
we feel a bit closer to you,
especially when we can't see you play.

Dreams Are All I Have

I want you to want me: like I want you;
but to you I'm just a fan
and you don't know who I am:
I wanna be the one you give your love to.

Dreams are all I have, sometimes I feel so sad;
I'm the one you're gonna give your love to.

I dream about you day and night,
I want your arms to hold me tight
but my dreams are the only way I can have you.

When I dream I kiss you, how I wish it *was* true:
I want your hands to walk round my body;
but you're so far away; I know it's true to say,
I want your love but I'll always be without it.

Dreams are all I have, sometimes I feel so sad;
I wanna be the one you give your love to.

Unknown Love

What kind of love is this
I feel for you; I crave your kiss.
Never have I felt so much
for a man I've never touched.

It's not just unrequited,
my love for you's unknown,
in a sea of other fans
but feeling so alone.

Wanting you to notice me,
some contact from afar,
will you remember my messages
or even my 'Good Luck' cards?

When you answered my question it thrilled me
to think that you'd read my e-mail:
it made me feel somehow closer
to you, my ideal male.

Do you even know that I exist?
Do you know how often I dream we've kissed?
Or how much I want to be part of your life?
If my dreams were real I'd be your wife.

The Fans' Wishes

Rafa, our love for you is limitless,
our wish for you, we give you this:
a mind full of joy and possibilities,
a heart full of faith in your abilities;
a voice filled with laughter till infinity,
a smile that lights up the vicinity;
a body that's fit as can be,
so your tennis will be carefree.

Sidetracked

Watching you play is a feast for the eyes,
"Vamos Rafa," the crowd all cries:
they call you 'Box office'
as you draw in the crowd;
the fans shout your name,
so loud and so proud;
you're the one we all want to see,
whether it's 'live' or on our TV;
you strike the ball so clean and true
and the way you look is striking too:
beautiful to watch, poetry in motion,
would you employ me
to apply your sun tan lotion?
I'm getting sidetracked now
but who can blame me?
You're the most beautiful man
that's been on my TV;
back to your tennis,
what strength and what power –
but my mind goes off track
and I need a cold shower!
Rafa you were put on this Earth to delight,
you do it for me, all day and all night!

Stress Less

In England when tired or stressed
we drink endless cups of tea,
but I don't think it would work for you
the way it works for me;

cos you said that you don't drink tea
when I asked you in 'The Times,'
so how about a hot chocolate
to help you to unwind!

One Track Mind

As I settle down to watch TV,
your face looks at me
from my mug of tea;
whatever film I'm watching,
I imagine you're the star,
whoever you replace,
you're the best by far.

In Romeo and Juliet,
if you took the lead,
I'd watch it so much,
my addiction I'd feed.
If you played Robin Hood
on a trusty old stallion,
in my mind, it's me
that's your true love,
Maid Marion.

As Tarzan in a loin cloth
you'd swing through the trees,
I'd get the part of Jane
as I wouldn't ask for fees!
If you played a baddie,
I'd still fall for you –
but there'd have to be lots of kissing
as that's in the contract too!

If they were casting for a soap opera
and need a sexy Spaniard,
after you they'd look no further,
you're of the highest standard!

If you were in a soap
three or four times a week,
immediately the ratings would soar
and reach their highest peak!

In the movies you'd look the best
whatever film you do,
and we'd all still be here
swooning over you!

A Meeting of Minds

When I'm sitting drinking tea,
from my Rafa mug,
I wonder what you're doing
as I sit upon the rug.

I wish that I was psychic
and could see you through the day,
knowing what you're doing,
knowing you're ok.

To have a small connection,
to feel closer to you,
to know you're feeling happy
or to help if you feel blue.

If in some way our minds could meet
and talk telepathically, that'd be neat!

Dreams of Rafa

He turned up on my doorstep one day,
I was so surprised and blown away!
I let him in, we took a seat,
then we had a bite to eat.

Laying in the sun on golden sands,
then a walk by the sea, holding hands;
a trip in a boat, far out to sea,
all alone, him and me.

It turns to dusk, the stars all shine,
he holds me close, his lips meet mine:
I love him and he loves me,
this is the perfect place to be;
but things aren't always what they seem,
the alarm goes off, it's just a dream!

Food for Thought

Imagine how amazing it would be
if Rafa posted on forums like you and me:
he could be anyone, an alias he'd use,
I'm going insane, searching for clues!

Someone who doesn't post very much
but nevertheless wants to stay in touch;
he could have himself on his avatar pic,
if we knew which one's him
we'd PM him quick!

There I go, getting carried away
but it adds excitement to a boring day,
so Rafa if you're out there too,
let us know which one is you!

TVE Interview

Rafa, I watched your interview on TVE tonight,
I was so enthralled I couldn't let you outta my sight:
with your mannerisms, charisma and angelic smile,
looking tanned and relaxed on your beautiful Isle.

It was a treat to glimpse at your fitness training,
to watch the gains that you are making,
and the beautiful body you've worked so hard for:
I had to rewind and watch it some more!

I couldn't understand much of the communication
so I'm on the computer to find the translation;
your interview, Rafa, was a joy to see,
things are looking good for you and your knee!

A Teenager's Daydream

Would Rafa Nadal notice me?
Would he take me home for a cuppa tea?
Would his eyes meet mine across the court?
Would he like the present that I've bought?
Would he throw his headband straight at me?
Would he invite me round his house for tea?

He'd take me home; we'd sit and eat;
across the table, our eyes would meet:
fixed in his gaze, I'd drown in his eyes,
next we're kissing: hear my sighs;
Oh Rafa – look what you do to me
as I sit and dream with my cup of tea!

What Would I Do?

Rafa, I love you, oh...so much,
what I would do, just to feel your touch:

I'd walk on hot coals to be where you are,
speed round a track in a fast racing car;

fly to the moon in a big shiny rocket,
just to feel your hand in my pocket!

To walk along with your hand on my arse –
Rafa, that would be first class!

Mid Life Madness

They say when you're an OAP
2nd childhood hits – just wait and see,
but what they all forget to tell you
is middle age plays havoc too;
mid life crisis, the ticking clock,
teen mentality comes as a shock:
a crush on a star just half your age,
your life is at a funny stage;
in your mind you feel like a teen
but your body reminds you,
it's well past sixteen!

Rafa's the one I've fallen for badly,
I love that guy, truly; deeply; madly.
I gaze at him with my rose coloured glasses
and dream that one day he'll make passes
at a woman who's teens ended in 84 –
I don't think it's against the law!
He was born in eighty six
when I was out partying getting my kicks –
but stranger things have happened in life,
he might like an older wife.

I'm sure that I could fit the bill,
you see I'm not quite over the hill:
I'm tiny and slender
and there's not much grey,
now I'm getting carried away!
But would he understand me,
I'm cockney through and through,
but with the language of love

I'm sure we'd get through;
and I can speak proper, if needs be,
I can't have Rafa not understanding me!

That man you see, really lights my candle,
he really is too hot to handle;
but I know I'd have a real good try,
if he asked me out, I'd feel so high;
he could just ignore my crooked neck,
kiss it better, what the heck!
I'm sure I'd soon forget it too,
with Rafa there I'd feel like new:
he'd whisper some romantic Spanish
so all my problems seem to vanish!

He's so mature; I'm young at heart,
we're made for each other, we'd never part:
he'd marry me; I'd be his wife,
I know we'd have a happy life;
it's not my body that's gone it's my head,
I've just remembered – I'm already wed!

My husband thinks I've lost my mind
but it's not something I want to find!
Rafa you see makes me feel sixteen
but in reality it's just a dream –
and it's one that many others have too,
so we're in good company, me and you.
Now I've come back down to earth with a thud,
I'd better go and peel the spuds!

The More We Know the More We Love

Because you're in the public eye,
as fans we feel we know you:
reading everything you say,
all the details about your play:
the more we know
the more we love,
you're the one we're dreaming of.

It's not because you're famous,
it's not because you're rich:
I'd still feel the same
if you worked for Highway Maintenance
and had to dig a ditch!

If I'd got to know you
working in a local shop,
I'd be mesmerized by your beauty:
my jaw it would still drop!

The reason that we love you
is for the person that you are:
kind and considerate,
loving and giving,
a man with good morals
who works hard for a living.

A man who wants to improve the world,
a man with a vision to make dreams unfurl;
a man full of goodness,
overflowing with love,
who makes people happy,

he's been sent from above.

Childlike yet mature,
young yet wise:
the ability to see
through others eyes.

Full of empathy
your feelings are deep:
you care for others,
your understanding's unique.

Each fan that loves you
feels just the same,
and it's nothing to do
with your money or fame.

Carried Away but Keeping it Real

You're not mine and I'm not yours
so I dream of you behind closed doors.
I love you, it's true;
I know what I'd like to do –
but you're taken and so am I,
maybe in another lifetime
I'll catch your eye.
My love for you feels exciting and new
but in reality I still love my husband too;
he buys me mags if you're front page
and jokes I'm at a funny age!
In this life I wish you well:
I want happiness for you,
can't you tell?
In this lifetime you've found your love,
maybe next time it'll be me you dream of,
and if I'm lucky, we'll be together
in another lifetime, for ever and ever!
There're many different kinds of love:
I love you from afar
for the person that you are;
I love you for your beauty
outside and in
and for the way you work so hard
and always aim to win.
I've never been to see you play,
I hope I will on some fine day:
to meet the man who's so elite
would really make my life complete.
Carried away but keeping it real
describes exactly how I feel.

Routines – Yours and Ours

Before each match you have your routines,
taping fingers, practice and focused on dreams;

well we have routines before you play too,
so when you're on TV, we're all stuck like glue!

We get all our chores done so they're outta the way,
but more important are the prayers,
that for you we say:

to Archangel Raphael so you'll stay fit and feel fine,
and to Apollo so your game is sublime,

to Serapis Bey for motivation so it's second to none,
so we've helped all we can Rafa –
you're our No.1.

"Dearest Apollo and Serapis Bay,
please help Rafa win today;
Dear Archangel Raphael,
please keep him strong, fit,
healthy and well."

Talking Toronto (with Rafa Quotes)

We hope you enjoyed your holiday
and are feeling relaxed and refreshed,
and are able to continue your 'A game,'
to leave your opponents perplexed!

This wish comes all the way from England
as we're sending you our love and support,
with lots of loud cheers;
in Canada your ears
will hear when you walk onto court!

We know you're fit and raring to go,
"the body is perfect,"
that we know!

"I can think about my tennis and not my body;"
we'll think about both Rafa – you're such a hottie!

"I'm a more com-plete player on all surfraces;"
we love your Spanglish –
it brings a smile to our faces!

If I Won

If I won the lottery
there would be no dichotomy:
I'd buy a Winnebago
and dress myself in dayglow;

I'd drive where Rafa goes,
and sit in the front rows;
he'd notice me from head to toes,
how could he not in dayglow clothes!

I'd cheer him on in rhyme
so he'd know it's me each time;
a different rhyme for every match
so at the end, his eye I'd catch,
hoping his wristband flies my way,
the perfect end to a perfect day!

My King of Clay

My 'King of Clay' will win today,
that's why he's called 'The King of Clay.'

He's a cut above the rest,
Rafa Nadal – you are the best!

You bring joy to all your fans
watching you is *always* in our plans.

You're the highlight of my day,
I just love to see you play.

When you're interviewed and I hear you speak,
you really make my legs go weak!

I'll always be your biggest fan,
Rafa Nadal, you're a wonderful man!

Rafa's 24th

Twenty four candles
to blow out this year,

but now your hair's shorter
you need have no fear:

even though the candles
are burning so bright,

there's not much chance
that your hair will ignite!

When you blow out those candles,
I'll be thinking of you,
hoping your birthday wishes come true.

Vamos Rafa

V is for Vamos, let the battle commence,
A is for Arm, you flex it real tense,
M is for Motivated,
O is for Optimist,
S is for Self-improvement, you always persist.

R is for Racket, the tool of your trade,
A is for Aims and the goals you have made,
F is for Fans and our feelings for you,
A is for Absent, when you are, we feel blue.

Rafa our hero, we think you're so fine,
when you're back on court, it'll be sublime.

I'm on Pins, Hoping You'll Win

I'm wishing you lots of luck from over the sea,
I'll be cheering you on as I watch my TV,

hoping and praying it's you that wins;
if the matches are close, it's like I'm on pins!

I walk round the room and 'Vamos' when you do,
oh Rafa, I feel what you feel too;

your fans are with you through every minute –
sending good vibes and hoping you win it.

The Many Sides of Rafa

I love you from your head down to your toes,
every day my love for you grows:
so many things about you
have made me feel this way,
if I tried to list them,
it'd take me half the day!

Sometimes at a press conference
there's that cute shy look at the floor:
that 'little boy lost' look, we all adore.
You have the smile of an angel,
so radiant, so bright,
it could warm the coldest heart
and make everything seem right.

Sometimes you're mischievous
with a sparkle in your eye:
seeing you laughing and joking
makes me feel so high.
On court you look muscular,
powerful and tough
yet your movements are elegant
and artistic – not rough.

In my book that's the perfect combination,
it explains why I feel such adulation;
I even love your hands
and the way you bounce the ball,
some men's are like bananas,
I don't like theirs at all!
Theirs are short and stubby

but yours are lithe and lean,
they're like your perfect body,
it really is pristine!

You've got a girl you love and trust,
she's not just a pretty face,
and every single one of us
would love to take her place!
But seriously, Rafa,
don't think it bizarre,
we want you to be happy
so we'll love you from afar!

Mesmerizing, charismatic, intoxicating & hot,
thinking about Rafa, I just can't stop,
all these things rolled into one man,
explain why he has so many fans!

Who?

Who's the most exciting player?
Who has the guts of a dragon slayer?

Who's a good influence on young and old?
Who's caring and compassionate with a heart of gold?

Who won International Spaniard?
Who has a character of the highest standard?

Who's won 14 grand slams?
Who's the one with the most loyal fans?

Rafael Nadal of course!

New Year – Picked Up More than a Trophy

You picked up a trophy beating Fed in Abu Dhabi,
but you also picked up a virus
that you couldn't shake; sadly,
in Doha you were so ill, you lost in the semi –
what you really needed was a good flu remedy!

You changed ya shirt 6 times,
you sweated so much on court;
this year; for you; bad luck it brought.

Then in Australia,
a hamstring injury stopped things being fine:
it stopped your chance
to try and hold all four slams at one time.

It's not been a very lucky start to your year
but Rafa your fans will always be here,
cheering you on, supporting *only* you;
we're not fair-weather fans,
we're here through storms too!

Good Luck for Aussie Open (2009)

You won Toronto on Hard Court
and Olympic Gold too,
you're a man with a mission –
they can't stop you.

You're well prepared
and fresh as a fish,
I hope you'll win
and get your wish.

I'll be cheering you on
from my sofa in the U.K.,
hoping that everything
goes your way!

Your tennis is spectacular,
the opponents know it too,
you're playing so well,
they can't stop you.

When you feel the breeze on your cheek
from over the sea,
in the wind are 'Good Luck' kisses,
to you – from me.
From England to Australia,
I send my love:
as you're the one
I'm thinking of.

French Open (May 23rd 2010)

Rafa, you're a master of your craft:
you got there through skill and a lot of hard graft;
mixing power and exquisite touch;
another trophy, you aim to clutch;
you've got millions of fans all hoping you will:
if you win back your trophy we'll all be so thrilled.

Now we have two weeks of nail biting tension:
we need a remedy for anxiety prevention,
but we all aim to stay calm, just like you,
you're determined and fit,
I'm sure you'll pull through;

and in two weeks when the final day dawns,
you'll be the winner when you lock horns;
you're our Spanish bull, our magical Mallorcan,
you let your tennis do the talking –
and talk it does, with flair and style,
you'll beat the others by a mile!

We're on Your Side

Good Luck Rafa, I hope you do well,
I'm rooting for you, I'm sure you can tell;
believe in yourself; let that inner fire roar,
block out the doubters and show them the door!

Strengthen your talents, stay focused and calm,
you'll soon be 'vamosing' and flexing your arm!
Don't listen to pressure, it's just sabotage:
just listen to the words of your own entourage.

Your millions of fans are cheering, it's true,
remember we all want the best for you.

If the crowd ever give you, a really rough ride,
in homes round the world, you've got us on your side:
even if us fans, in the crowd, can't be,
we're all round the world, with you on our TV:
cheering you on from our sofa's at home,
remember that always, if you're feeling alone.

If some people like to see you knocked down,
remember us true fans, we're always around,
we want to help you to feel calm and sure
that you've got what it takes, to win more and more.

When you're happy, we're happy,
when you're sad we are too,
we feel what you feel: we're part of it too,
so if we can help you by letting you know,
we're all on your side, we love you, you know!

ESPY Award for Rafa

The best male tennis player won an ESPY Award,
Rafa that's you and your fans will applaud,
to congratulate and cheer you
in all that you do,
what a deserving winner,
I'm so glad it was you!

You have so many qualities,
it's you that appeals,
you're no pretender –
you're the real deal!

Congratulations Rafael
from Juliette;
I know there's lots more
of your best to come yet.

Good Luck for Wimbledon 2011 Rafa

Welcome back to Wimbledon,
we're so glad that you're here,
our defending champion,
for you we will cheer,
if you win again,
it'll be a dream come true,
not only for you
but for all your fans too.

The excitement is mounting,
we can't wait till it starts,
if the matches are close,
you'll hear all our hearts,
beating so loud,
it's torture we feel,
hoping you find
your opponents Achilles heel,
and beat him in four sets
or better still three,
so you're still full of vigour
and big energy!

I hope my poetry is a good luck charm,
so you'll be winning with ease
and flexing your arm,
shouting 'Vamos'
and playing your best

so all your opponents
don't pass the test,
when they come up against you,
you hit every ball back,
so they realise to beat you,
they don't have the knack –
soon they'll be on their way home;
they'd better go pack!

It goes without saying,
you've got my support,
I can't wait to see you
when you walk onto court,
so good luck for Wimbledon 2011,
I'll be cheering from Cornwall;
it's not far from Devon!

For Rafa on the Eve of Wimbledon 2011

Rafa's back on track
to claim his trophy back,
we give him our loyalty,
to us he's tennis Royalty;
it's a special occasion
and a tough rival he's playing
but Rafa's tennis is blazin' –
for Rafa we're praying
that all his serves stay in
and our nerves won't be fraying!

Rafa we know you can do it,
our support will help fuel it;
our positive vibes and energy
will help your tennis be the best it can be.

We feel that we share
every moment with you,
the bad, the good,
all the way through;
we hope the result
is another win for you
on the Wimbledon grass,
we love you, it's true.

Laureus Awards on TV (UK) 12/2/2011

For UK Rafa fans there's a treat in store,
Saturday morning, don't go out your door,

switch on the TV at 11.10
if you wanna see Rafa Nadal again!

Put on channel 5 for the Laureus awards
to see Rafa win the Best Sportsman – of course!

He's the best and it's been acknowledged again,
so join me in cheering our hero from Spain!

Rafa's 'Off the Hook'

You raced outta the blocks,
running at speed,
ripping the ball –
they'd better take heed:
the King's in town
and he's in great form,
all his opponents
will feel forlorn.
He's looking so strong,
sturdy and sure,
he races ahead,
then rips it some more!
Watching him play
is a joy to behold,
he's skillful, artistic,
courageous and bold.
He's utterly dominant
hitting winners ten a penny:
if you don't know my expression
it means 'very many;'
when you play it's like a demo
of just what to do,
no one else does it better,
because they're not you.
As well as all that
we love how you look,
you're the sexiest athlete,
you're so 'off the hook'.

Enthralled

Enthralled
by every move he makes;
mesmerizing –
my breath he takes
away from me,
I gasp and stare,
Rafa is beyond compare.

Sexy shots
in the zone,
focused intent,
never roam:
complete control,
accurate and sharp,
acute angles,
bites worse than bark;
determined,
like a whirlwind –
match under belt,
first blow's been dealt.

Down But Not Out!

Well-equipped warrior,
sexy and cute,
for ever I'll follow you,
along any route.
Every match you play
I'm with you in spirit;
from my sofa in the UK:
hoping you'll win it!
Nail-biting tension,
then I let out a cry,
"Vamos Rafa,"
with relief, I sigh;
you were down for a while
but certainly not out:
you found the solution –
now Berdych is out!

More Wins Ahoy

Rafael,
for you I fell:
my tears well,
tears of joy,
your face so coy,
trophy ahoy;
Spanish boy –
more wins ahoy!

Watching Rafa Play

At the start of the match when the coin is bounced
he's like a lion, waiting to pounce:
agile, powerful and in control,
confident that he'll reach his goal.

During the match, he's focused and calm,
he hits a winner and flexes his arm;
I'm on the sofa, but right there with him,
just as elated with each point he wins;
hunky, muscular sexy and strong,
I could watch this man all day long.

When he's concentrating hard
he looks smouldering and tough,
oozing sex appeal, I can't get enough;
then when he wins, he falls to the ground,
the deserving winner, makes my heart pound,
biting the trophy with a gleam in his eye,
beaming and sexy – that's my guy!

I'm With You Every Point

My heart and my head are there with you,
every point you play, I feel it too,
I love to watch every move you make,
mannerisms, topspin shots, you look so great;

the concentration when you serve an ace
like a sexy trance on your beautiful face;
it's true other players have talent too,
but they're not as pleasing to the eye as you;

your groundstrokes move them side to side,
they can't get the ball and their hopes have died;
fast and swift to the net, you put away a volley,
sweat drips from your rival, he craves an ice lolly;

it won't be long before he can get one,
cos very soon the match'll be won –
by you Rafa!

Rafa's Chainsaw Massacre

When he's on his way to winning
and he's really in the zone,
his involuntary reaction
shows his satisfaction.

Rafael, vamos some more,
do the chainsaw,
it's a very good score.

He's such a lovely mover,
we watch him with delight,
when he does the chainsaw
he sets the crowd alight!

When you see him do it,
you can be very sure,
it's Rafa's chainsaw massacre:
his opponent's on the floor!

It could be made into a dance move
with a song all of its own,
as a battle cry for Rafa fans,
all around the globe.

We can do it at the tournaments,
we can do it from our homes,
we can take it to the nightclubs
and everywhere we roam.

Here's my little song,
I hope you'll sing along,

give Rafa your support
whenever he's on court.

During the match,
he's in the zone,
reflex reaction,
shows satisfaction.
Vamos some more,
do the chainsaw,
hit the dance floor!

It's the Rafa move,
get into the groove,
if you're a Rafa fan,
on your feet, stand;
hit the dance floor
and do the chainsaw!

Up the intensity,
show 'em who's boss,
raise your leg up
and shout 'Vamos;'
synchronize your bicep,
flex your arm,
it's the chainsaw massacre
but he's still full of charm!

Rafael, vamos some more,
do the chainsaw,
we love ya forever more!

Davis Cup Tennis

Davis Cup Tennis
has a great atmosphere,
the band playing loudly
and the fans they all cheer;
it's all so exciting, even on my TV,
I want Spain to win –
they're my favourite you see.
You might think it strange
that I don't support the U.K.
but it's you that I love –
what more can I say!
In a past life
I think I must have been Spanish:
vague memories in my soul,
they'll never vanish.

After the Match

When the match was over
he shook his hair around the place,
it was sexy and unruly,
hanging all around his face.

It really looked so sexy,
my heart it skipped a beat
and his famous arse was just 1st class,
I'm nearly fainting at his feet!

Then with a sexy look,
his eyes they glanced my way,
his voice spoke exotic 'Spanglish,'
it really made my day!

Then when he held the trophy,
his teeth, they took a bite,
perhaps his tummy's rumbling
after such a lengthy fight!

Another Award

Another Award, Rafael,
you're so valued, I can tell.
Well deserved,
like every ace you served:
due to hard work,
you never shirk –
it's been observed.

Our Hungry Warrior

Rafa Nadal, you're loved by so many,
you're a warrior on court with a fire in your belly:
you give your best, you always do,
we admire you so much, our feelings are true.

We wish you good luck whenever you play,
your fans support is here to stay:
we'll always be here, on your side,
cheering you on, bursting with pride.

Good Luck for the World Tour Finals

I've asked the Spiritual Sporting Guru's
Apollo and Serapis Bey,
to help you win and pave the way,
for a wonderful end to a difficult year,
to help you get in a winning gear:
then you'll be the one they're failing to beat
and you'll be the last man on your feet!

Good Luck Rafa; my prayers are with you,
so you feel fit, well and confident too;
if the amount of good vibes sent
affect the outcome,
then for sure, you'll be the winning one
as you have more fans than the rest,
in our eyes, you'll always be the best!

World Tour Finals, Fans' Feelings

This poem is written just for you:
no one else moves me the way that you do;
there are other good players
who just 'say' the right thing,
with you it's genuine – compassion you bring.
I feel with some of the others, it's all PR,
but with you it's real – you raise the bar:
they just say what they feel they ought to,
but you're full of empathy – they're just not you.

People see inside you a soul that is true,
you're somebody special; we see that in you;
and on court your 'never say die' attitude
is something that you always exude.
You've had problems this year
but you're back fighting again:
more respect and admiration
is what you have gained;
to get a win now, the climb feels steeper,
but when you do, it'll be much sweeter.

You never give up – that you refuse,
you always make us proud if you win or lose;
we share your emotions, the ups and the downs,
but never forget, we're always around –
like extended family, we want the best for you,
we want to help you get it
so all your dreams come true.

Fan Aid

Trust your instincts and intuition,
you'll move forward and gain fruition
and fulfillment of your plans –
your destiny is in your hands.

A few changes could bring the results you crave:
you know in your heart which ones will aid,
your plans to win will then come true
because of a few adjustments by you.

Maybe you need to be more aggressive and bold
like when you won Olympic Gold:
just remember and visualize how you felt then –
no one could beat you,
you believed you would win.

At Wimbledon you believed, you were on a roll,
nothing could stop you reaching your goal;
I know the more wins you have,
the easier it becomes,
lets start today with a winning run!

Your fans are all behind you and will be for ever:
we want to help you with this endeavour;
we hope that everything goes in your favour
and you have a great win that you can savour.

To Rafael from Juliette

I love the way your shorts fit
tight around your quadriceps,
I wish you had no shirt sleeves
so I could see more of your biceps;
who is this I'm crazy about?
Rafa Nadal of course:
when you're on telly I vamos so much
I sometimes end up hoarse!

Rafa I wish I could clone you
so that we all can get our share
of your Spanish charm and lovely smile –
if I knew how to, I really would dare!

To Rafael from Juliette,
my poems for you are not done yet;
you're so inspiring, I keep on writing,
my thoughts and feelings are igniting!
Fireworks are going off in my brain
because I'm thinking of you again!

(watch this space!)

About the Author

I've loved tennis since I was 6,
I watched it on my TV;
my first hero was Chris Evert-Lloyd
like her, I wanted to be.

Conners, Nastase, Agassi, Cash,
I got up early and to Wimbledon did dash;
I queued for hours and just got in,
standing room on the centre court,
but Pat Cash didn't win!

The Benson and Hedges Championships at Wembley
with Cash, Yanik Noah and McEnroe,
but I left my car lights on all day
so when I left, I couldn't go!

I rang my friend Sue,
she came to the rescue:
she gave me a jump start
so from Wembley I could depart!

I've watched the Wimbledon Final on TV every year
and for me something became very clear,
from the first moment I saw him, I wanted him to win,
I've been a true fan of Rafa's –
my favourite is him!

Feedback Appreciated on Amazon

What is a poem?
A poem is words that sound pleasing together
but a meaning is something that I must endeavour,
to put into it, to make it complete,
it all has to fit; be succinct and neat,
it must be in language we all use today
not highbrow stuff,
where you don't understand what I say,
it must strike a chord, make you identify with it,
and enjoy reading my words so you don't wanna quit
half way through, and leave it in limbo,
not knowing where the ending will go;
so if you've stayed with me
I've done my job well,
if you wanna read another,
your friends then, please tell!

Index

Lightning Source UK Ltd.
Milton Keynes UK
UKOW06f1032240516

274877UK00003B/152/P